APANESE
menu

6 languages ··········

Guide to authentic Japanese cuisine
Guide de l'authentique cuisine japonaise
Ihr Ratgeber für japanische Küche
Guida all'autentica cucina giapponese
Guía de la auténtica cocina japonesa
Guia da autêntica comida japonêsa

En Ⓥ= vegan version usually available
Ⓕ Ⓥ= existe aussi en version végétalienne
Ⓓ Ⓥ= veganische Variante meistens auch erhäl
Ⓘ Ⓥ= di solito la versione vegan è disponibile
Es Ⓥ= se suele ofrecer también una versión vegetal
Ⓟ Ⓥ= poderá ser vegetariana

ASHIMI

さしみ

Raw fish & shellfish
fish / shellfish

Only served very fresh. Eat at start of meal to enjoy the delicate flavours, dipped in mix of **shōyu** and **wasabi**.

Poisson et fruits de mer crus
poisson / fruits de mer

Toujours servi très frais. A déguster en début de repas, avec un mélange de **shōyu** et de **wasabi**.

Roher Fisch & rohe Muscheln
Fisch / Meeresfrüchte

Wird ganz frisch serviert. Gut als Vorspeiser, getunkt in eine Mischung aus **Shōyu** und **Wasabi**.

Pesce e molluschi crudi
pesce / frutti di mare

Mangiato solo freschissimo all'inizio del pasto per gustare i sapori delicati, inzuppato in un misto di **shōyu** e **wasabi**.

Pescado y marisco crudo
pescado / marisco

Se come muy fresco como entrante para disfrutar de su delicado sabor. Se unta en **shōyu** y **wasabi**.

Peixe e marisco cru
peixe / marisco

Servido apenas muito fresco. Molhe em **shōyu** e **wasabi** e coma no início da refeição, para apreciar o sabor.

Seafood & rice fingers
fish / shellfish Ⓥ

Slivers of fish and shellfish, cooked or raw, served on sweet vinegared rice, often with **wasabi**. Dip in **shōyu**.

Bouchées de poisson et de riz
poisson / fruits de mer Ⓥ

Copeaux de poissons et de fruits de mer, cuits ou crus, sur riz au vinaigre, souvent avec **wasabi**. A tremper dans du **shōyu**.

Roher Fisch auf Reis
Fisch / Meeresfrüchte Ⓥ

Meeresfrüchte oder Fisch, roh oder gekocht, auf mariniertem Reis, oft mit **Wasabi**. In **Shōyu** tunken.

Bastoncini di pesce e riso
pesce / frutti di mare Ⓥ

Listelle di pesce e mollusco cotti o crudi serviti su riso dolce all'aceto, spesso con **wasabi**. Inzuppare in **shōyu**.

Delicias de marisco y pescado
pescado / marisco Ⓥ

Tiras de pescado y marisco, crudo o cocinado, con arroz agridulce y **wasabi**. Se untan en **shōyu**.

Marisco e rolinhos de arroz
peixe / marisco Ⓥ

Lascas de peixe ou mariscos cozindos ou crus, c/ arroz de vinagre doce, às vezes c/ **wasabi**. Molhe em **shōyu**.

TEMPURA

天ぷら

Japanese fritters
fish / shellfish

Seafood or vegetables in crispy egg batter. Dip in radish and **ten-tsuyu** mix, or just add salt and lemon.

Beignets japonais
poisson / fruits de mer

Beignets de fruits de mer ou légumes. A tremper dans un mélange de radis et **ten-tsuyu** ou assaisonner avec sel et citron.

Backteighappen
Fisch / Meeresfrüchte

Meeresfrüchte oder Gemüse in Backteig. In Rettich und **Ten-tsuyu** tunken oder mit Salz und Zitrone essen.

Frittelle giapponesi
pesce / frutti di mare

Frutti di mare o verdure in pastella croccante. Inzuppare in un misto di ravanelli e **ten-tsuyu** o solo sale e limone.

Frituras japonesas
pescado / marisco

Marisco o verdura con gabardina crujiente. Se untan en una mezcla de rábano y **ten-tsuyu**, o se les pone sal y limón.

Frituras japonesas
peixe / marisco

Marisco ou legumes fritos. Molhe em mistura de rabanete e **ten-tsuyu** ou junte sal e limão.

AKI-TORI

Charcoal-grilled chicken
meat
Skewers of choice morsels, grilled with **tare** or salt, and sprinkled with **shichimi**. Typical with evening drinks.

Poulet grillé sur charbon de bois
viande
Brochettes de poulet grillé, avec **tare** ou sel, parfois servi avec **shichimi**. Amuse-gueule typique.

Huhn vom Holzkohlengrill
Fleisch
Spießchen, mit **Tare** oder Salz gegrillt, oft mit **Shichimi** bestreut. Meist am Abend zu Drinks serviert.

Pollo alla brace
carne
Spiedini di squisiti bocconi alla brace con **tare** o sale, si possono spolverare di **shichimi**. Tipico con drink serali.

Pollo a la parrilla
carne
Brochetas de trozos a elegir, asados con **tare** o sal, y rociados de **shichimi**. Se suelen tomar por la noche, con las copas.

Espetadas de frango na brasa
carne
Espetadas grelhadas com **tare** ou sal, podem ser salpicadas com **shichimi**. Comum com bebidas à noite.

RI NO TERI-YAKI

鰤の照り焼き

Glaze-grilled yellowtail
meat / fish
Fish steak basted in **shōyu**, **mirin**, **sake** and sugar. Slightly sweet. Chicken **teri-yaki** also very popular.

Sériole grillée avec glaçage
viande / poisson
Steak de poisson enduit de **shōyu**, **mirin**, **sake** et sucre. La version poulet est aussi très populaire.

Gegrillter, glasierter Gelbschwanz
Fleisch / Fisch
Fischsteak in **Shōyu**, **Mirin**, **Sake** und Zucker. Leicht süß. Ebenfalls beliebt ist Huhn **Teri-yaki**.

Seriola glassata alla griglia
carne / pesce
Porzioni dolciastre di pesce coperte di **shōyu**, **mirin**, **sake** e zucchero. Popolare è anche il pollo **teri-yaki**.

Sorel glaseado a la parrilla
carne / pescado
Filete de pescado (o pollo) untado en **shōyu**, **mirin**, **sake** y azúcar. Sabor ligeramente dulce.

Linguado grelhado na chapa
carne / peixe
Posta cozida em **shōyu**, **mirin**, aguardente de arroz e açúcar. Adoçada. O **teri-yaki** de frango também é muito popular.

12

NMA NO SHIO-YAKI

さんまの塩焼き

Salt-grilled saury
fish
Tasty autumn fish prepared by simple, classic method. Salt keeps flesh moist and enhances natural flavour.

Orphie maquereau en croûte de sel
poisson
Recette simple et classique très goûteuse. Poisson d'automne savoureux et moelleux enrobé dans sa couche de sel.

Salzgegrillter Makrelenhecht
Fisch
Schmackhafter Herbstfisch, klassisch zubereitet. Salz erhält den Fisch saftig und betont den Geschmack.

Gastaurello al sale grigliato
pesce
Pesce autunnale saporito preparato in modo classico. Il sale lo mantiene umido e valorizza il sapore naturale.

Paparda asada a la sal
pescado
Sabroso pescado de otoño. La sal mantiene la carne jugosa y realza su delicado sabor.

Tira-vira grelhado no sal
peixe
Saboroso peixe de Outono, preparado de modo simples e clássico. O sal mantém a carne húmida e saborosa.

BUTA NO SHŌGA-YAKI

豚の生姜焼き

Pork & ginger stir-fry
meat
Fried with **shōyu**, **sake**, **mirin** and ginger. Sweet and succulent. Good lunch with shredded cabbage.

Sauté de porc au gingembre
viande
Frit avec **shōyu**, **sake**, **mirin** et gingembre. Délicat et succulent. Délicieux déjeuner avec émincé de choux.

Kurz gebratenes Schweinefleisch
Fleisch
Mit **Shōyu**, **Sake**, **Mirin** und Ingwer gebraten. Süß u. saftig. Gut als Mittagessen mit gehobeltem Kraut.

Maiale saltato con zenzero
carne
Fritto nel **shōyu**, **sake**, **mirin** e zenzero. Dolce e succulento è un bel pranzo con julienne di cavolo.

Fritura de cerdo y jengibre
carne
Frito con **shōyu**, **sake**, **mirin** y jengibre. Dulce y suculento. Con col rallada, ideal para la comida.

Porco & gengibre salteados
carne
Frito em **shōyu**, gengibre, **mirin** e aguardente de arroz. Doce e suculento. Bom almoço com couve em juliana.

鉄板焼き

Griddled steak
meat / fish / shellfish
Theatrically fried at table with vegetables and **tare**. American-Japanese fusion dish, also made with fish.

Steak frit sur plaque en fonte
viande / poisson / fruits de mer
Frit devant convives avec légumes et **tare**. Recette américano-japonaise, existe aussi en version poisson.

Grillsteak
Fleisch / Fisch / Meeresfrüchte
Amerikanisch-japanische Speise, bei Tisch gebraten, mit Gemüse und **Tare**. Auch mit Fisch erhältlich.

Braciola grigliata
carne / pesce / frutti di mare
Fritta a tavola, per effetto, con verdura e **tare**. Unione di americano e giapponese, è fatto anche con pesce.

Bistec a la plancha
carne / pescado / marisco
Se asa en la misma mesa con verduras y **tare**. Plato americano y japonés, también se hace con pescado.

Bife grelhado
carne / peixe / marisco
Preparado na mesa com legumes e **tare**. Prato de fusão américo-japonesa, também feito com peixe.

KONOMI-YAKI

お好み焼き

As you like it pancake
meat / shellfish
Choice of savoury ingredients in batter. Fried at table, brushed with sauce, and garnished generously.

Crêpe fantaisie
viande / fruits de mer
Crêpes aux divers ingrédients salés, préparées devant les convives, avec sauce et abondante garniture.

Omelett nach Wunsch
Fleisch / Meeresfrüchte
Salzige Zutaten nach Wunsch in Backteig. Bei Tisch gebraten, mit Soße überzogen, üppig garniert.

Frittella salata, a scelta
carne / frutti di mare
Ingredienti salati di vostra scelta in una pastella. Fritta al tavolo, spalmata di salsa e guarnita generosamente.

Torta al gusto
carne / pescado
Masa a la que se añaden sabrosos ingredientes. Las tortas se preparan en la mesa y se untan con salsa.

Panqueca a gosto
carne / marisco
Poderá fazer com diversos ingredientes. Frita à mesa, pincelada com molho e guarnecida generosamente.

TON-KATSU

とんかつ

Breaded pork cutlet
meat
Deep-fried and served with shredded cabbage and special thick brown sauce. A popular lunch.

Côtelette de porc panée
viande
Frit et servi avec éminçé de choux et une épaisse sauce brune spéciale. Constitue aussi un déjeuner populaire.

Paniertes Schweinskotelett
Fleisch
Frittiert, als Beilage gehobeltes Kraut. Wird mit dicker brauner Soße serviert. Beliebtes Mittagessen.

Cotoletta impanata di maiale
carne
Cotoletta fritta e servita con julienne di cavolo ed una speciale salsa scura. Apprezzata a pranzo.

Costilla de cerdo rebozada
carne
Se fríe en aceite y se sirve con col rallada y una salsa marrón espesa. Buena opción al mediodía.

Costeleta de porco panada
carne
Frita e servida com couve juliana e um molho castanho espesso especial. É um almoço popular.

USHI-AGE

Breaded kebabs
meat / fish / shellfish

Seafood, vegetables or meat, deep-fried and very tasty. Add favourite sauce, and bite from skewer.

Brochettes frites
viande / poisson / fruits de mer

Fruits de mer, légumes ou viande frits et très goûtés. Servi avec sauce de son choix, sur la brochette.

Panierte Spieße
Fleisch / Fisch / Meeresfrüchte

Meeresfrüchte, Gemüse oder Fleisch, frittiert, voller Geschmack. Lieblingssoße dazu und vom Spieß essen.

Spiedini impanati
carne / pesce / frutti di mare

Saporiti frutti di mare, carne e verdura fritti. Aggiungete la vostra salsa preferita e mangiate direttamente dallo spiedino.

Pinchos rebozados
carne / pescado / marisco

Marisco, hortalizas o carne fritos y muy sabrosos. Untar en la salsa preferida y morder del mismo pincho.

Espetadas panadas
carne / peixe / marisco

Marisco, legumes ou carne fritos e saborosos. Junte o seu molho favorito e coma a partir do espeto.

YOSE-NABE

寄せ鍋

Mixed hotpot
meat / fish / shellfish

Chef's choice of seafood, meat and vegetables simmered in rich stock at the table. Add delicate items last.

Potée variée
viande / poisson / fruits de mer

Sélection de fruits de mer, ou viande et légumes, mijotée devant les convives dans riche bouillon.

Gemischter Eintopf
Fleisch / Fisch / Meeresfrüchte

Vom Koch ausgewählte Zutaten in reichhaltiger Brühe bei Tisch gekocht, besonders zarte Stücke zuletzt.

Spezzatino misto
carne / pesce / frutti di mare

Frutti di mare, carne e verdure scelte dello chef cotte al tavolo nel brodo. Aggiungete le cose delicate per ultime.

Cocido variado
carne / pescado / marisco

Selección del chef, de marisco, carne y hortalizas. Se cuecen en un caldo concentrado, en la misma mesa.

Cozido misto
carne / peixe / marisco

Escolha feita pelo chefe de carne, legumes e marisco, cozidos em caldo rico. Feito à mesa.

SUKI-YAKI

すき焼き

B eef hotpot
meat
Beef slices browned and simmered in sauce, with vegetables and **shirataki**, at table. Dip in beaten egg to eat.

R agoût de bœuf
viande
Fines tranches de bœuf mijotées devant les convives dans sauce aux légumes et **shirataki**. A plonger dans œuf battu.

R indfleischeintopf
Fleisch
Rindfleisch, bei Tisch mit Gemüse und **Shirataki** in Soße gegart. Zum Essen in geschlagenes Ei tauchen.

S pezzatino di manzo
carne
Fettine di carne rosolate e sobbollite al tavolo in salsa con verdure e **shirataki**. Si mangia inzuppato in uovo sbattuto.

C ocido de ternera
carne
Rodajas finas de ternera doradas y hervidas en salsa, con verdura y **shirataki**. Se cuecen en la mesa y se untan en huevo.

G uisado de vaca
carne
Fatias de carne alouradas e cozidas em molho, com **shirataki** e legumes, na mesa. Molhe em ovo batido.

しゃぶしゃぶ

Beef fondue
meat

Named for the sound of beef swished in stock. Dip in **ponzu** or sesame sauce to eat. Can finish with **udon**.

Fondue de bœuf
viande

Nommé d'après le son du bœuf tourné dans bouillon. A tremper dans **ponzu** ou sauce au sésame. Parfois servi avec **udon**.

Rindfleischfondue
Fleisch

Rindfleischscheiben in Brühe gekocht. In **Ponzu** oder Sesamsoße tunken. Zuletzt evtl. **Udon** beifügen.

Fonduta di manzo
carne

Nome simile al suono della carne nel brodo. Si mangia inzuppata in **ponzu** o salsa di sesamo. Potete finire con **udon**.

Fondue de ternera
carne

El nombre alude al sonido que hace la carne al agitarla en el caldo. Untar en **ponzu** o salsa de sésamo.

Fondue de vaca
carne

Nome derivado do som da carne mergulhada no caldo. Molhe em **ponzu** ou molho de sésamo. Termine com **udon**.

ODEN

おでん

Hodge podge
meat / fish / gluten

Stewed hotpot. Wide choice includes fishballs, radish, **konnyaku** and boiled eggs. Served with mustard.

Salmigondis
viande / poisson / gluten

Ragoût composé entre autres de boulettes de poissons, radis, **konnyaku** et œufs durs. Servi avec moutarde.

Eintopf
Fleisch / Fisch / Gluten

Viele verschiedene Zutaten: Fischbällchen, Rettich, **Konnyaku** und gekochte Eier. Mit Senf serviert.

Miscuglio di cose
carne / pesce / glutine

Stufato misto. Ampia scelta, fra cui polpette di pesce, ravanello, **konnyaku** e uova sode. Servito con mostarda.

Cocido mixto
carne / pescado / gluten

Cocido con gran variedad de ingredientes: rábano, bolitas de pescado, **konnyaku** y huevo duro. Se sirve con mostaza.

Mistura
carne / peixe / glúten

Estufada. Escolha variada: rabanetes, bolas de peixe, **konnyaku** e ovos cozidos. Servida com mostarda.

ATSU-DON

Bowl of deep-fried pork meat
Ton-katsu soaked in egg, half-poached in sweet broth with onions, and served on rice. Common filling lunch.

Bol de porc frit viande
Ton-katsu trempé dans de l'œuf à peine poché dans bouillon sucré aux oignons. Servi sur lit de riz.

Schweinefleischschüssel Fleisch
Ton-katsu, in Ei getaucht, in süßer Brühe mit Zwiebeln pochiert, auf Reis. Beliebtes, sättigendes Mittagessen.

Ciotola di maiale fritto carne
Ton-katsu imbevuto in uovo, scottato in brodo dolce con cipolle e servito su riso. Pranzo comune e saziante.

Bol con cerdo frito carne
Ton-katsu untado en huevo, semiescalfado en caldo dulce con cebolla. Se sirve acompañado de arroz.

Taça de porco frito carne
Ton-katsu molhado em ovo, escalfado em molho doce com cebolas e servido sobre arroz. Almoço substancial.

YŪ-DON

牛 丼

Bowl of beef
meat
Slivers of beef and
onion lightly simmered in
sweet broth and all poured
over large bowl of rice.

Bol de bœuf
viande
Domburi simple. Copeaux
de bœuf et d'oignons mijotés
dans bouillon sucré et servis
sur grand bol de riz.

Rindsschüssel
Fleisch
Rindfleisch- und
Zwiebelscheiben, in süßer
Brühe gekocht, über eine
große Schale Reis gegossen.

Ciotola di manzo
carne
Listelle di manzo
e cipolle appena sobbollite
in brodo dolce, rovesciate su
una grande ciotola di riso.

Bol de carne de ternera
carne
Tiras de ternera y
cebolla cocidas a fuego lento
en caldo dulce. Se sirve con
un buen bol de arroz.

Taça de carne de vaca
carne
Tiras de carne de vaca
e cebola cozidas em molho
adocicado e vertidas sobre
uma grande taça de arroz.

YAKO-DON

親子丼

Parent & child bowl
meat

Named for the chicken pieces and beaten egg, lightly cooked with onions in broth and served on rice.

Bol du parent et de son enfant
viande

Nommé d'après les morceaux de poulet et l'œuf battu, mijotés avec oignons et servis sur lit de riz.

Eltern-Kind-Schüssel
Fleisch

Hühnerfleischstücke (Eltern) und geschlagenes Ei (Kind) werden mit Zwiebeln in Brühe gekocht und auf Reis serviert.

Ciotola chioccia e pulcino
carne

Prende il nome dai pezzi di pollo e dall'uovo sbattuto, appena cotti in brodo con cipolle e serviti su riso.

Bol "madre e hijo"
carne

Su nombre se debe a los trozos de pollo y al huevo batido cocidos en caldo con cebolla a fuego lento. Se sirve con arroz.

Taça de mãe e filho
carne

O nome vem da galinha e do seu filho "ovo" batido, cozido levemente. Servido sobra arroz.

NA-JŪ

Grilled eel in box
fish
Fillets charcoal-grilled with **tare** and served with rice in lacquer box. Sprinkle with bitter **sanshō**.

Boîte contenant anguille grillée
poisson
Filets grillés sur charbon de bois avec **tare** et servis avec riz dans boîte laquée. A parsemer de **sanshō**.

Grillaal im Lackkästchen
Fisch
Aalfillet mit **Tare** vom Holzkohlengrill, m. Reis im Lackkästchen serviert. Mit bitterem **Sanshō** bestreuen.

Scatola di anguilla
pesce
Filetti grigliati alla brace con **tare** e serviti con riso in una scatola laccata. Spolverare con l'amaro **sanshō**.

Caja con anguila a la barbacoa
pescado
Filetes a la barbacoa con **tare**, se sirven con arroz en una caja de laca. Rociar con **sanshō** amargo.

Caixa de enguia grelhada
peixe
Filetes grelhados em carvão com **tare**, servidos com arroz em caixa de laca. Salpique com **sanshō** amargo.

きつねうどん

Fox's noodles
gluten

Hot broth with the sweet fried **tōfu** loved by the fox-god. Spice with **shichimi**. Also served as **soba** dish.

Nouilles du renard
gluten

Bouillon chaud avec **tōfu** frit, prédilection du dieu renard. Assaisonner de **shichimi**. Existe aussi en version **soba**.

Nudeln für den Fuchs
Gluten

Der Fuchsgott soll süß gebratenen **Tōfu** lieben. Mit **Shichimi** gewürzt, auch als **Soba**-Speise erhältlich.

Spaghettoni della volpe
glutine

Brodo caldo con **tōfu** dolce fritto, favorito dal dio-volpe. Aromatizzato con **shichimi**. Servito anche come piatto **soba**.

Fideos del dios-zorro
gluten

Caldo caliente con **tōfu** dulce frito; plato preferido del dios-zorro. Sazonar con **shichimi**. Puede hacerse con **soba**.

Massa de raposa
gluten

Caldo quente com **tōfu** doce frito, apreciado pelo deus raposa. Tempere com **shichimi**. Também é servido como **soba**.

ZARU-SOBA

Cold buckwheat noodles
gluten
Dip **soba** in cold **tsuyu** for refreshing summer dish. To finish, add hot noodle water to **tsuyu** and drink.

Nouilles de sarrasin froides
gluten
Soba trempé dans **tsuyu** froid, rafraîchissant l'été. Boire ensuite l'eau de cuisson chaude des nouilles ajoutée au **tsuyu**.

Kalte Buchweizennudeln
Gluten
Erfrischende Speise für den Sommer. **Soba** in kaltes **Tsuyu** tauchen. Zuletzt heißes Nudelwasser zufügen und trinken.

Spaghettini di grano saraceno
glutine
Inzuppate **soba** nel **tsuyu** freddo per un rinfrescante piatto estivo. Finite unendo l'acqua calda della pasta al **tsuyu** e bevete.

Fideos fríos de alforfón
gluten
Plato de verano, los **soba** se mojan en **tsuyu** frío, al que al final se le añade el agua caliente de hervir y se bebe todo junto.

Massa fria de trigo mourisco
glúten
Molhe **soba** em **tsuyu** frio para obter um prato refrescante. Para terminar, junte água quente de cozer a massa ao **tsuyu** e beba.

RĀMEN

ラーメン

Chinese egg noodles
meat / fish / gluten

Hot, meaty broth with roast pork, fishroll and bamboo. Other choices include wonton and bean sprouts.

Nouilles chinoises aux œufs
viande / poisson / gluten

Bouillon viandé chaud avec porc rôti, rouleaux de poisson et bambou. Existe aussi avec légumes sautés.

Chinesische Eiernudeln
Fleisch / Fisch / Gluten

Heiße Brühe mit Schweinebraten, Fischrolle und Bambus. Auch mit Wonton und Bohnensprossen möglich.

Spaghettini cinesi all'uovo.
carne / pesce / glutine

Brodo di carne caldo con maiale arrosto, rotoli di pesce e bambù. Altre scelte includono butti di fagioli e fagottini vari.

Fideos chinos de huevo
carne / pescado / gluten

Caldo caliente con cerdo asado al horno, rollitos de pescado y bambú. Otras versiones incluyen verduras sofritas.

Massa chinesa de ovos
carne / peixe / glúten

Caldo quente de carne c/ porco assado, rolinhos de peixe e bambu. Outras variedades: wantan e rebentos de feijão.

KARĒ-RAISU

カレーライス

Curry rice
meat / shellfish Ⓥ

Mild or hot spicy sauce, often left to develop flavour overnight. Introduced by 19th century British traders.

Riz au curry
viande / fruits de mer Ⓥ

Sauce peu ou très pimentée, souvent préparée la veille. Introduite par des Britanniques au 19ième siècle.

Curryreis
Fleisch / Meeresfrüchte Ⓥ

Mit milder oder scharfer Soße, wird zur Intensivierung des Geschmacks oft über Nacht stehen gelassen.

Riso al curry
carne / frutti di mare Ⓥ

Salsa semi-delicata o piccante spesso lasciata ad insaporire di notte. Introdotta nel 19° secolo da mercanti britannici.

Arroz al curry
carne / marisco Ⓥ

Salsa picante que se suele dejar reposar una noche para obtener un sabor más intenso. Origen anglo-indio.

Arroz de caril
carne / marisco Ⓥ

Molho pouco picante. Muitas vezes fica a marinar durante a noite. Introduzido no século XIX pelos Ingleses.

KIKOMI-GOHAN

炊き込み御飯

Boiled mixed rice
meat √

Seasonal vegetables, stock and often chicken, boiled gently with rice to infuse flavours. Eaten as main dish.

Plat de riz mijoté
viande √

Légumes de saison, bouillon et souvent poulet, longuement mijotés avec du riz. Plat principal.

Gekochter gemischter Reis
Fleisch √

Hauptspeise mit Gemüse der Saison, Brühe und Huhn. Für intensiven Geschmack lange mit dem Reis gekocht.

Riso misto bollito
carne √

Verdure di stagione, brodo e spesso pollo bolliti piano piano con riso per fondere i sapori. È un piatto principale.

Arroz hervido mixto
carne √

Plato principal. Verduras de temporada, caldo y a veces también pollo, hervido a fuego lento con arroz.

Arroz de mistura
carne √

Arroz de verdura nova, a que poderá juntar frango cozido ou marisco. Prato principal, muito delecioso.

CHA-ZUKE

お茶漬け

Savoury tea rice
fish √

Rice topped with shreds of fish or pickles and covered with delicate stock or green tea. Good after drinks.

Riz au thé
poisson √

Riz servi avec copeaux de poissons ou pickles et délicat bouillon ou thé vert. Agréable après de l'alcool.

Salziger Teereis
Fisch √

Reis, zerpflückter Fisch oder Pickles, mit zarter Brühe oder grünem Tee übergossen. Beliebt nach Drinks.

Riso su tè saporito
pesce √

Riso coperto da listelle di pesce o sottaceti e coperto con un delicato brodo o da tè verde. Buono dopo i drink.

Arroz al té
pescado √

Arroz con trozos de pescado o encurtidos, regado con un caldo fino o con té verde. Ideal para acompañar las bebidas.

Arroz com chá
peixe √

Arroz coberto com tiras de peixe ou pickles e regado com caldo delicado ou chá. Bom depois das bebidas.

茶碗蒸し

Savoury egg custard
meat / shellfish

Favourite side dish. Made with fish stock and often chicken, prawns or gingko nuts, and steamed to set.

Crème salée à base d'œuf
viande / fruits de mer

Plat d'accompagnement. Bouillon de poisson, souvent avec poulet, crevettes ou noix de gingko, cuits à la vapeur.

Salzige Eierspeise
Fleisch / Meeresfrüchte

Beliebte Beilage. Wird mit Fischbrühe, Huhn, Garnelen oder Gingkonüssen zubereitet und zum Stocken gedämpft.

Crema di uovo salata
carne / frutti di mare

Un contorno favorito. Fatta con brodo di pesce, spesso con pollo, gamberetti o noci di ginkgo e cotta a vapore.

Cuajada de huevo
carne / marisco

Entremés muy popular, con caldo de pescado y a veces pollo, gambas o nueces *gingko*, hecho al vapor hasta que cuaja.

Creme de ovo
carne / marisco

Feito c/ caldo de peixe e às vezes frango, gambas ou nozes de gincgo cozidos a vapor. Um dos acepipes favoritos.

SUNO-MONO

酢の物

Vinegared salads
fish / shellfish √
Served with **sake** or tea, as appetisers or to cleanse the palate. Delicacies include seaweeds and jellyfish.

Salades au vinaigre
poisson / fruits de mer √
Servies avec **sake** ou thé, en apéritif ou comme rafraîchissement. Raffinées avec algues ou méduse.

Marinierte Salate
Fisch / Meeresfrüchte √
Mit **Sake** oder Tee als Häppchen vor oder zwischen Gängen serviert. Beliebt sind Algen und Quallen.

Insalate all'aceto
pesce / frutti di mare √
Servite con **sake** o tea come antipasti o per pulire il palato. Fra le specialità sono incluse alghe e meduse.

Ensaladas con vinagreta
pescado / marisco √
Se sirven con **sake** o té, como aperitivo o entremés. Ingredientes singulares como algas y medusas.

Saladas com vinagre
peixe / marisco √
Servidas com **sake** ou chá, como aperitivo ou para limpar o palato. Acepipes incluem algas e acalefas.

SUIMONO & MISO-SHIRU

お吸い物・味噌汁

Soups
meat / gluten √

Clear, delicate **o-suimono** may include chicken stock. **Miso-shiru** is very savoury, often with **tōfu** or **wakame**.

Soupes
viande / gluten √

O-suimono limpides parfois à base de bouillon de poulet. **Miso-shiru** goûteux, comprenant souvent **tōfu** ou **wakame**.

Suppen
Fleisch / Gluten √

Klare, zarte **O-suimono** kann Huhn enthalten. **Miso-shiru** ist salzig und enthält oft **Tōfu** oder **Wakame**.

Minestre
carne / glutine √

L'**o-suimono**, consommé delicato, può includere brodo di pollo. **Miso-shiru** è saporito e spesso ha **tōfu** o **wakame**.

Sopas
carne / gluten √

Las **o-suimono** claras y suaves pueden ser a base de caldo de pollo. Las **miso-shiru** suelen llevar **tōfu** o **wakame**.

Sopas
carne / glúten √

As **o-suimono** delicadas podem incluir caldo de frango. A **miso-shiru** é saborosa e às vezes inclui **tōfu** ou **wakame**.

UKE-MONO

Pickles
√ Essential for any meal. Made with salt, vinegar, **sake** lees or rice bran, more for flavour than to preserve.

Pickles
√ Accompagnent tout repas. Préservés dans du sel, vinaigre, **sake** ou son de riz dont ils tirent leur goût.

Pickles
√ Wichtig bei jeder Mahlzeit. Aus Salz, Essig, **Sake** Trebern oder Reiskleie, intensiviert den Geschmack.

Sottaceti
√ Parte essenziale dei pasti. Fatti con sale, aceto, fondo di **sake** o crusca di riso, più per il sapore che per preservarli.

Encurtidos
√ Esenciales para acompañar cualquier comida. Se hacen con sal, vinagre, poso de **sake** o salvado de arroz.

Pickles
√ Essenciais numa refeição. Feitos com sal, vinagre, **sake** ou farelo de arroz, sobretudo pelo seu sabor.

SHŌKADŌ BENTŌ

松花堂弁当

C alligrapher's box
meat / fish / shellfish √

Haute cuisine of four different types of food. Named after 17th century artist, for paintbox shape.

B oîte du calligraphe
viande / poisson / fruits de mer √

Quatre types de nourriture très raffinée. Nommé d'après la boîte de couleurs d'un artiste du 17ième siècle.

K alligraphiekästchen
Fleisch / Fisch / Meeresfrüchte √

Feine Küche mit vier verschiedenen Speisen. Nach den Farbkästchen der Künstler im 17. Jh. benannt.

L attina del calligrafo
carne / pesce / frutti di mare √

Alta cucina di quattro diversi tipi di cibo. Prende il nome dall'artista del 17° secolo per la forma delle scatole dei colori.

C aja de caligrafía
carne / pescado / marisco √

Plato exquisito con cuatro tipos diferentes de comida. El nombre proviene de un calígrafo del siglo XVII.

C aixa do Caligrafista
carne / peixe / marisco √

Alta cozinha com quatro tipos diversos de comida. O nome deriva da caixa de tintas de um artista do século XVII.

O-ZENDATE

yaki-zakana

daikon-oroshi

1. o-cha 2. okazu 3. shōyu 4. tsuke-mono
5. gohan 6. miso-shiru 7. hashi

YAKUMI

wasabi

me-jiso · shiso

momiji-oroshi

nori

beni-shōga

shichimi

sanshō

64

日本食
NIHON-SHOKU

- **En** About Japanese food
- **F** Quelques mots sur la cuisine japonais
- **D** Wissenwertes über japanische Speisen
- **I** Parliamo dei cibo giapponese
- **Es** Todo sobre la comida japonesa
- **P** Tudo sobre comida japonêsa

- **En** Food & drink
- **F** Nourriture & boissons
- **D** Essen & Trinken
- **I** Cibi & bevande
- **Es** Comida & bebida
- **P** Comida & bebida

食事

ENGLISH

Tiny ornamental delicacies, filling winter hotpots, or deep-fried pork cutlets: the Japanese menu provides for every taste and occasion. Meeting for a meal or drinks is the typical way to socialise in Japan, and an evening's drinking is always accompanied by small dishes or nibbles, often finished with a rice dish like **o-cha-zuke**. A meal is often accompanied or followed by complimentary green tea, to cleanse the palate, and at an expensive restaurant the staple white rice should be included without charge. But wherever you eat the staff will take pride in their hospitality and service.

FRANÇAIS

Mets délicats minuscules, ragoûts consistants ou côtes de porc frites: le menu japonais s'adapte à tous les goûts et à toutes les occasions. Il est courant au Japon de se retrouver autour d'un repas ou d'un verre. Le soir, la consommation d'alcool est toujours accompagnée d'une collation, et se termine souvent par un plat de riz tel que **o-cha-zuke**. Le restaurant vous offre parfois du thé vert, agréable au fin de repas pour rafraîchir le palais et dans un restaurant de luxe, du riz au naturel est normalement inclu dans le prix. Cependant, quel que soit le lieu de restauration, le personnel tire fierté de l'hospitalité et de la qualité du service qui vous sont offerts.

DEUTSCH

Winzige, dekorative Delikatessen, sättigende Wintereintöpfe, frittierte Schweinskoteletts – die japanische Speisekarte hat für jeden Geschmack und Anlaß etwas bereit. Gewöhnlich trifft man sich in Japan zum Essen oder auf einen Drink, zudem immer kleine Häppchen oder Knabbereien serviert werden, als Abschluss oft auch ein Reisgericht wie **O-cha-zuke**. Mahlzeiten werden oft von grünem Tee begleitet oder abgeschlossen, um den Gaumen zu reinigen. Der Tee ist oft im Preis enthalten, in feinen Restaurants gilt dies auch für den weißen Reis. Wo immer Sie essen, das Personal wird sich bemühen, Gastlichkeit und guten Service zu bieten.

ITALIANO

Piccole specialità di guarnizione, stufati invernali che saziano o cotolette di maiale fritte: il menù giapponese provvede per tutti gusti e tutte le occasioni. Incontrarsi per mangiare o prendere dei drink è il modo tipico di socializzare in Giappone e i drink alla sera sono sempre accompagnati da piccoli piatti o snack, spesso guarniti con un piatto di riso come il **o-cha-zuke**. Il pasto viene spesso accompagnato o seguito da tè verde con i complimenti della casa per pulire il palato e in un ristorante caro il riso bianco semplice dovrebbe essere incluso nel prezzo. Dovunque mangerete lo staff si presenterà comunque ospitale ed efficiente.

ESPAÑOL

De diminutas exquisiteces ornamentales hasta opulentos cocidos invernales, pasando por chuletas de cerdo fritas, la cocina japonesa ofrece platos para todos los gustos y ocasiones. En Japón, la vida social suele ir estrechamente vinculada a la gastronomía, y junto con los refrescos o las copas que se sale a tomar por la noche se sirven siempre tapas y aperitivos, culminados al final con un plato de arroz como el **o-cha-zuke**. Para beber durante o después de la comida, muchos locales ofrecen por sistema té verde, ideal para limpiar el paladar. Por regla general, los restaurantes de categoría no cobran el arroz blanco de acompañamiento. El común denominador de todos los locales de restauración japoneses es el servicio, siempre amable y atento.

PORTUGUÊS

Pequenos acepipes ornamentais, estufados substanciais para o Inverno ou costeletas de porco fritas: a cozinha japonesa satisfaz qualquer paladar em qualquer ocasião. Reunir-se com as pessoas para uma refeição ou para uma bebida é o modo tradicional de conviver no Japão. Tomar uma bebida à noite implica sempre comer pequenos pratos ou petiscos, muitas vezes terminando com um prato de arroz como o **o-cha-zuke**. Uma refeição é quase sempre acompanhada por chá (grátis), para limpar o palato, e num restaurante caro o arroz branco que tem um lugar central deve estar incluído no preço da refeição. Mas, seja qual for o local em que coma, todo o pessoal terá orgulho em oferecer o melhor serviço e hospitalidade.

- **En** Structure of a meal
- **F** Organisation du repas
- **D** Menüzusammenstellung
- **I** Come si svolge un pasto
- **Es** Composicion de la comida
- **P** A estrutura de uma refeição

ENGLISH

Meals come in many shapes, from Western steak with salad to a single bowl of noodles, but the classic format is rice, soup, pickles and **okazu** (dishes), all served at once. A simple lunch might have one okazu, while the traditional breakfast includes grilled fish, raw egg and sheets of **nori**. Dinner could feature two or three okazu, arriving while your **zensai** (appetisers) are still on the table. Many places serve little **o-tōshi** to acknowledge your order, and soup is typically **o-suimono** or **miso-shiru**. Dessert options, if any, might include green tea ice cream or fruit.

FRANÇAIS

Toutes sortes de repas sont servis, allant du steak-salade à l'occidentale à un simple bol de nouilles, mais le repas classique comprend du riz, de la soupe, des pickles et **okazu** (plats) présentés ensemble. Un déjeuner simple peut ne comporter qu'un seul okazu, tandis que le petit-déjeuner traditionnel comprend du poisson grillé, un œuf cru et des feuilles de **nori**. Le dîner peut comprendre deux ou trois okazu qui sont servis alors que vos **zensai** (apéritifs) sont encore sur la table. Beaucoup de restaurants servent de petits **o-tōshi** pour vous aider à patienter et **o-suimono** ou **miso-shiru** sont les soupes les plus typiques. Le choix de dessert se limite souvent à de la glace au thé vert ou à des fruits.

DEUTSCH

Mahlzeiten können viele Formen annehmen, Steak und Salat wie im Westen oder auch nur eine Schüssel Nudeln, doch das klassische Format besteht aus Reis, Suppe, Pickles und **Okazu** (Speisen), die alle gleichzeitig serviert werden. Ein einfaches Mittagessen enthält vielleicht nur eine Okazu, während zum traditionellen Frühstück gegrillte Fische, rohes Ei und **Nori**-Blätter gehören. Ein Abendessen enthält zwei oder drei Okazu, die schon serviert werden, wenn die **Zensai** (Häppchen) noch auf dem Tisch stehen. Viele Gaststätten servieren kleine **O-tōshi**, um Ihre Bestellung zu bestätigen, und als Suppe häufig **O-suimono** oder **Miso-shiru**. Als Nachspeise, so vorhande, wird oft Eis aus grünem Tee oder Obst angeboten.

ITALIANO

I pasti possono essere di diversi tipi, dall'occidentale bistecca con contorno di insalata ad una ciotola unica di tagliolini, ma il formato classico è composto da riso, minestra, sottaceti e **okazu** (piatti) serviti tutti insieme. Un pranzo semplice può limitarsi ad un okazu mentre la colazione tradizionale include pesci alla griglia, uovo crudo e sfoglie di **nori**. La cena potrebbe presentare due o tre okazu che arrivano mentre i vostri **zensai** (antipasti) sono sempre sul tavolo. Molti ristoranti servono piccoli **o-tōshi** come riconoscimento del fatto che avete ordinato. La minestra di solito è **o-suimono** o **miso-shiru** e il dessert può, in caso, includere tè verde, gelato o frutta.

ESPAÑOL

Los menús son de lo más dispares, desde un bistec con ensalada, al estilo occidental hasta un simple bol de fideos. Sin embargo, la composición habitual incluye arroz, sopa, encurtidos y **okazu** (platos), todo a la vez. Un almuerzo simple puede constar solamente de un okazu, mientras que el desayuno tradicional se compone de pescado a la plancha, huevo crudo y láminas de **nori**. La cena puede comprender dos o tres okazu, que se sirven mientras todavía se están tomando los **zensai** (aperitivos). Muchos locales sirven pequeños **o-tōshi** como muestra de atención al cliente. En cuanto a la sopa, se toma **o-suimono** o **miso-shiru**. Si el restaurante tiene carta de postres, que no siempre es el caso, suele incluir helado de té verde o fruta.

PORTUGUÊS

As refeições assumem diversas formas, desde o bife com salada tipicamente ocidental a uma simples taça de massa, mas o formato clássico inclui arroz, sopa, pickles e **okazu** (pratos), tudo servido em simultâneo. Um almoço simples pode conter um okazu, enquanto que o pequeno-almoço tradicional inclui peixe grelhado, ovo cru e folhas de **nori**. O jantar pode consistir de dois ou três okazu, que são servidos enquanto os **zensai** (aperitivos) ainda estão na mesa. Em muitos locais é servido algum **o-tōshi** enquanto o seu pedido é preparado. A sopa é tipicamente **o-suimono** ou **miso-shiru** e a sobremesa, quando existe, pode incluir gelado de chá verde ou fruta.

- **En** Where to eat
- **F** Choix de restaurants
- **D** Wohin zum Essen
- **I** Dove si mangia
- **Es** Tipos de restaurantes
- **P** Onde comer

場所

ENGLISH

Restaurants vary from the haute cuisine **ryō-tei**, to **shoku-dō** and **teishoku-ya** serving good, cheap set meals, while the popular department store restaurants stay open into the evening offering a little of everything. For the expert touch, however, try a specialist eatery. **Unagi-ya** serve eel and loach, and noodle shops divide into **rāmen-ya** and **soba-ya** (where most dishes are also made with **udon**). **Ton-katsu-ya** and **sushi-ya** are popular for lunchtime or evening, and after five o'clock red lanterns invite customers into **nomi-ya** and cheap, friendly **izaka-ya** for drinks with snacks like **yaki-tori**.

FRANÇAIS

La gamme de restaurants s'étend des **ryō-tei** servant de la haute cuisine, aux **shoku-dō** et aux **teishoku-ya** qui offrent des menus fixes bon marché mais de qualité tandis que les restaurants des grands magasins, ouverts tard le soir, proposent un peu de tout. Pour une cuisine plus spécialisée, essayez les restaurants à thème. **Unagi-ya** sert de l'anguille et de la loche et les restaurants de nouilles sont divisés en **rāmen-ya** et en **soba-ya** (où la plupart des plats sont aussi à base de **udon**). **Ton-katsu-ya** et **sushi-ya** sont populaires à l'heure du déjeuner ou le soir. Dans la soirée, des lanternes rouges incitent les clients à entrer dans les **nomi-ya** et dans de conviviaux **izaka-ya** pour boire un verre autour de collations telles que les **yaki-tori**.

DEUTSCH

Das Restaurantangebot ist vielfältig, von feinster Küche in einem **Ryō-tei** hin zu **Shoku-dō** und **Teishoku-ya**, wo man gute, preisgünstige Menüs findet. Die beliebten Kaufhausrestaurants haben bis in den Abend hinein offen und bieten von allem etwas. Eine besondere Erfahrung sind jedoch Spezialitätenrestaurants. **Unagi-ya** bieten Aal und Schmerle an, Nudelgeschäfte werden unterteilt in **Rāmen-ya** und **Soba-ya** (wo die meisten Gerichte auch mit **Udon** zubereitet werden). **Ton-katsu-ya** und **Sushi-ya** sind mittags und abends beliebt. Nach 17 Uhr laden rote Latemen Gäste in **Nomi-ya** und billige, gemütliche **Izaka-ya** ein, wo man Getränke und kleine Knabbereien wie **Yaki-tori** konsumiert.

ITALIANO

I ristoranti variano da quelli di alta cucina **ryō-tei** al **shoku-dō** ed al **teishoku-ya** che servono pasti fissi buoni e a buon prezzo, ea quelli popolari di grandi magazzini che restano aperti fino a sera ed offrono un po' di tutto. Per fruire del tocco dell'esperto però, è meglio trovare un posto specializzato. Gli **unagi-ya** servono anguilla e pesce-barometro ed i negozi di pasta si dividono in **rāmen-ya** e **soba-ya** (dove la maggior parte dei piatti sono anche fatti con **udon**). **Ton-katsu-ya** e **sushi-ya** sono favoriti a pranzo o la sera, e dopo le cinque di pomeriggio lanterne rosse invitano i clienti ad entrare nei simpatici e poco cari **nomi-ya** ed **izaka-ya** per drink con snack come **yaki-tori**.

ESPAÑOL

Los restaurantes japoneses varían desde los más selectos, llamados **ryō-tei**, hasta los **shoku-dō** y los **teishoku-ya**, que sirven platos combinados sabrosos y económicos. Los locales de los grandes almacenes, muy populares, permanecen abiertos hasta la noche y ofrecen un poco de todo, sin embargo, los paladares más exigentes preferirán degustar la cocina de los locales especializados. Los **unagi-ya** sirven anguila y locha, y los locales de pasta se dividen entre **rāmen-ya** y **soba-ya** (casi todos los platos están hechos con **udon**). A los **ton-katsu-ya** y **sushi-ya** se va tanto al mediodía como por la noche, y después de las cinco de la tarde se encienden las luces rojas invitando a la clientela a los **nomi-ya** y los **izaka-ya**, donde se sirven refrescos con tapas como el **yaki-tori**.

PORTUGUÊS

Os restaurantes disponíveis vão desde a alta cozinha **ryō-tei** até ao **shoku-dō** e **teishoku-ya** que servem ementas fixas boas e económicas, enquanto os populares restaurantes dos centros comerciais, que estão abertos até mais tarde, oferecem um pouco de tudo. Os **unagi-ya** servem enguia e pardelha e os locais especializados em massas dividem-se em **rāmen-ya** e **soba-ya** (onde a maioria dos pratos também é confeccionada com **udon**). Os **ton-katsu-ya** e os **sushi-ya** são típicos em almoços e jantares e, depois das cinco horas, as lanternas vermelhas convidam os clientes a entrar nos **nomi-ya** (nas tascas) e nos **izaka-ya** (nas tabernas); ou nos **yaki-tori-ya** (tapas bares).

En In the restaurant
F Au restaurant
D Im Restaurant
I Al ristorante
Es En el restaurante
P No restaurante

ENGLISH

Staff should greet you on arrival, but if a casual restaurant is busy just grab a seat. At formal places it is polite to reserve, and some secluded **ryō-tei** require a personal introduction, but the traditional **tatami** room can also be enjoyed even in some **soba-ya**: leave your shoes on the step and kneel on the rush mats, or dangle your feet in a well under the low table. Men may sit cross-legged, at their host's invitation. At the end, pay at the till – tax may be additional to the prices shown. Personal tipping is not done, but at expensive restaurants a service charge is added to the bill.

FRANÇAIS

Le personnel doit normalement vous accueillir à l'entrée, mais dans un restaurant bon marché vous pouvez vous installer directement. Dans un lieu formel, il est poli de réserver, et l'admission à certains **ryō-tei** exclusifs se fait uniquement sur recommandation. Des salles de **tatami** sont disponibles dans les **ryō-tei**, ainsi que dans certains **soba-ya**: laissez vos chaussures à l'entrée et agenouillez-vous sur les nattes à la table basse. Les hommes s'assoient les jambes croisées sur invitation de leur hôte. Réglez l'addition en fin de repas; la TVA n'est parfois pas comprise dans les prix. Laisser un pourboire ne se fait pas, mais les grands restaurants ajoutent parfois le service.

DEUTSCH

Beim Eintreffen werden Sie normalerweise begrüßt, aber wenn in einem weniger formellen Restaurant gerade viel Betrieb ist, suchen Sie sich einfach einen Platz. In feinen Restaurants ist es höflich, einen Tisch zu bestellen, und für besonders exklusive **Ryō-tei** ist eine persönliche Empfehlung nötig. Im traditionellen **Tatami**-Zimmer, das Sie nicht nur in feinen **Ryō-tei** finden, können Sie auf Schilfmatten beim niedrigen Tisch knien. Männer dürfen auch im Schneidersitz sitzen. Bezahlen Sie am Ende, zu den angeführten Preisen kommt u.U. noch Steuer hinzu. Trinkgeld ist nicht üblich, doch kommt in teuren Restaurants ein Servicebeitrag zur Rechnung hinzu.

ITALIANO

Lo staff vi saluterà al vostro arrivo ma se in un ristorante casuale c'è molta gente, prendetevi pure una sedia. In un luogo formale è bene prenotare ed è necessario essere presentati personalmente per alcuni dei più ricercati **ryō-tei** ma la tradizionale stanza **tatami** può essere anche goduta in alcuni **soba-ya**:– lasciate pure le scarpe alla porta e inginocchiatevi sul tappetino di giunco o dondolate i piedi nel grosso incavo sotto la tavola così bassa. Gli uomini possono sedere a gambe incrociate, solo su invito del loro ospite. Alla fine pagate alla cassa – è possibile che talvolta venga aggiunta una tassa ai prezzi. La mancia personale non è da farsi, ma nei ristoranti ricercati il servizio è aggiunto al conto.

ESPAÑOL

Normalmente el camarero recibe a los comensales, pero si se trata de un restaurante sencillo y el personal está ocupado puede elegir usted la mesa. En locales más refinados es mejor reservar, y para algunos **ryō-tei** requiere una recomendación personal de otro cliente. A veces, en algunos **soba-ya** también se puede disfrutar de la tradicional sala **tatami**: deje los zapatos en el umbral y arrodíllese en las esterillas de junco trenzado. No está mal visto que los hombres se sienten con las piernas cruzadas. Una vez finalizada la comida, pase por caja a pagar, y tenga en cuenta que a veces aún se tienen que sumar los impuestos a los precios indicados en la nota. No se le da propina al personal, pero los restaurantes caros añaden un importe determinado en concepto de servicio.

PORTUGUÊS

Os empregados devem dar-lhe as boas-vindas mas, se estiver num restaurante informal com muito movimento, sente-se onde quiser. Nos locais mais formais é sinal de boa-educação fazer reservas antecipadas e alguns **ryō-tei** mais exclusivos exigem uma apresentação pessoal, mas a sala de **tatami** tradicional também pode ser apreciada mesmo em alguns **soba-ya**: deixe os sapatos à entrada e ajoelhe-se nas esteiras ou coloque os pés no espaço disponível por baixo da pequena mesa. Os homens podem sentar-se de pernas cruzadas, se o anfitrião os convidar a fazê-lo. No final, pague na caixa – pode haver uma taxa adicional sobre os preços apresentados. Não é costume serem dadas gorjetas mas nalguns restaurantes caros terá de pagar pelo serviço.

注文

- 🇬🇧 How to order
- 🇫🇷 Comment commander
- 🇩🇪 Die Bestellung
- 🇮🇹 Come ordinare
- 🇪🇸 Cómo pedir la comida
- 🇵🇹 Como pedir

ENGLISH

Ordering is easy. Many casual restaurants display life-like models of the day's **setto ranchi** (set lunches) or **teishoku** (any set meal) – just point and ask for, "Aré, o kudasai." At a **tempura-ya** sets are graded **ume**, **take**, **matsu** (literally apricot, bamboo, pine) while **sushi-ya** offer **nami**, **jō** and **toku-jō** from basic to extra-special. Haute cuisine meals too tend to be chosen by the chef, to use the freshest seasonal ingredients. Otherwise, an à la carte menu is usually available. Choose a variety of differently cooked dishes for a classic balanced meal.

FRANÇAIS

Il est facile de passer commande. Beaucoup de restaurants populaires exhibent des maquettes du **setto ranchi** (déjeuner du jour) ou du **teishoku** (tout menu fixe). Il vous suffit d'en montrer un du doigt en disant "Aré, o kudasai". À un **tempura-ya**, les menus sont classés **ume**, **take**, **matsu** (littéralement abricot, bambou, pin) tandis les **sushi-ya** proposent **nami**, **jō** et **toku-jō**, allant de l'ordinaire au menu raffiné. Les menus de haute cuisine tendent aussi à être sélectionnés par le chef pour utiliser les ingrédients les plus frais de la saison. Un menu à la carte est également toujours disponible. Composez votre menu avec différents types de plats pour avoir un repas classique équilibré.

DEUTSCH

Bestellen ist nicht schwer. Viele einfache Restaurants haben Modelle der **Setto ranchi** (Tagesmenüs für Mittagessen) oder **Teishoku** (Menüs) ausgestellt – zeigen Sie einfach darauf und sagen Sie, "Are, o kudasai." In einem **Tempura-ya** rangieren die Menüs von **Ume** über **Take** zu **Matsu** (wörtl. Aprikose, Bambus, Kiefer), und ein **Sushi-ya** bietet **Nami**, **Jō** und **Toku-jō** in der Rangfolge von einfach bis hin zu ganz besonders. Mahlzeiten der gehobenen Küche werden meist vom Küchenchef zusammengestellt, der die frischesten Zutaten der Saison kombiniert. Ansonsten ist gewöhnlich eine à la carte Auswahl vorhanden. Wenn Sie eine klassische, ausgewogene Mahlzeit zusammenstellen wollen, wählen Sie Gerichte, die auf verschiedene Weise zubereitet wurden.

ITALIANO

Ordinare è facile. In molti ristoranti informali ci sono modelli a grandezza naturale del **setto ranchi** (pasti fissi) del giorno o del **teishoku** (pasto fisso qualsiasi) – basta che indicate con il dito e diciate: "Arè, o kudasai." Ad un **tempura-ya** i pasti fissi sono classificati come **ume**, **take**, **matsu** (lett. albicocca, bambù, pino) mentre i **sushi-ya** offrono **nami**, **jō** e **toku-jō** dalla versione di base a quella extra speciale. Anche i piatti di alta cucina di solito vengono scelti dallo chef al fine di usare i più freschi ingredienti di stagione; altrimenti di solito è possibile chiedere un menù alla carta. Scegliete comunque una varietà di piatti differenti cotti in modo diverso per un pasto classico bilanciato.

ESPAÑOL

En muchos restaurantes se exponen ejemplos de los **setto ranchi** ("almuerzos del día") o **teishoku** (cualquier otro plato combinado), o sea que no tiene más que señalar el que quiera comer, diciendo "Aré, o kudasai." En los **tempura-ya** se han clasificado los menús por categorías, **ume**, **take** y **matsu** (que literalmente significan albaricoque, bambú, pino), mientras que los **sushi-ya** distinguen desde el menú básico hasta el especial entre **nami**, **jō** y **toku-jō**. En los locales de postín, lo normal es que sea el maître el que escoja la comida, para seleccionar los ingredientes más frescos y del tiempo. Sin embargo, también se puede comer a la carta. Se recomienda optar por diversos platos cocinados de maneras diferentes, componiendo así un menú clásico y equilibrado.

PORTUGUÊS

Fazer um pedido é fácil. Muitos restaurantes informais têm modelos do **setto ranchi** do dia (pratos do dia) ou **teishoku** (qualquer ementa fixa) – limite-se a apontar e a dizer: "Are, o kudasai." Num **tempura-ya** os pratos estão classificados segundo **ume**, **take**, **matsu** (literalmente alperce, bambu, pinheiro) enquanto o **sushi-ya** oferece **nami**, **jō** e **toku-jō**, do básico ao especial. As refeições de alta cozinha também quase sempre seleccionadas pelo chefe, para que sejam utilizados os ingredientes mais frescos da época. No entanto, em geral existe uma ementa à escolha. Opte por pratos confeccionados de forma variada para obter uma refeição clássica equilibrada.

- 🇬🇧 Communal dishes
- 🇫🇷 Plats collectifs
- 🇩🇪 Gerichte für mehrere Personen
- 🇮🇹 Piatti comuni
- 🇪🇸 Platos compartidos
- 🇵🇹 Pratos colectivos

ENGLISH

Most meals arrive in a collection of small personal servings, though friends may pick from the same dish with the back ends of their chopsticks, but a few communal dishes are convivially cooked at the table. The winter favourites, **nabe-mono**, simmer on a charcoal brazier while you add ingredients to keep the pot going. The secret is not to cook too much at once – but still politely finish all, so check the minimum number served. Staff are always on hand to assist, and for **teppan-yaki** will dramatically stir-fry at your table. The inset **teppan** (iron griddle) is also used to fry **okonomi-yaki**.

FRANÇAIS

La plupart des repas sont servis en petites portions individuelles, mais entre amis on peut se servir dans le même plat en utilisant la partie arrière de ses baguettes. Certains plats collectifs sont cuisinés par les convives à même la table. Parmi les plats classiques d'hiver, figure le **nabe-mono** qui mijote sur un brasier de charbon de bois et auquel on ajoute au fur et à mesure des ingrédients. Il est poli de ne pas se servir de trop grosses quantités à la fois. N'oubliez pas non plus de vérifier le nombre minimum de convives requis. Le personnel est toujours prêt à aider, et pour le plat de **teppan-yaki** fait sauter les ingrédients avec panache à votre table. Le **teppan** (plaque de fonte) incrusté dans la table est également utilisé pour faire frire **okonomi-yaki**.

DEUTSCH

Die meisten Mahlzeiten werden in kleinen Einzelportionen serviert, doch können sich Freunde mit dem hinteren Ende ihrer Eßstäbchen aus Ihrem Schüsselchen bedienen. Einige wenige Gerichte werden jedoch gemeinsam bei Tisch zubereitet. Beliebte Wintereintöpfe wie **Nabe-mono** köcheln über einem Holzkohlenfeuer, und Sie fügen Zutaten zum Topf hinzu und halten ihn so im Gang. Der Trick ist der, nicht zu viel auf einmal zu kochen und doch höflich alles aufzuessen. Prüfen Sie daher die Mindest-personenanzahl für das Gericht. Das Personal ist gerne bereit, bei der Zubereitung zu helfen, und beim **Teppan-yaki** wird die Speise dramatisch bei Tisch unter Rühren schnell gebraten. Die eingebaute Eisenplatte **Teppan** dient außerdem dazu, **Okonomi-yaki** zu garen.

ITALIANO

La maggior parte dei piatti arriva sotto forma di un insieme di porzioncine personali anche se fra amici è permesso assaggiare dallo stesso piatto con il dietro dei propri bastoncini ma ci sono alcuni piatti comuni che vengono cotti al tavolo per aumentare la giovialità. I piatti favoriti nell'inverno, i **nabe-mono**, sobbollono sulla brace mentre aggiungete ingredienti per non far interrompere la cottura nella pentola. Il segreto è di non far cuocere troppo tutto insieme, ma allo stesso tempo finire tutto; quindi è il caso che controllate il minimo numero di persone che saranno servite. Lo staff è sempre disponibile ad assistervi e il **teppan-yaki** addirittura viene saltato con teatralità sul vostro tavolo. La **teppan** (piastra di ferro) è anche usata per friggere l'**okonomi-yaki.**

ESPAÑOL

La mayoría de comidas se presentan en platos individuales, aunque si se tienen amistad los comensales pueden picar del mismo plato utilizando los extremos opuestos de los palillos. Sin embargo, hay otro tipo de platos compartidos que se cocinan en la misma mesa, en un ambiente relajado y jovial. Los favoritos para el invierno, **nabe-mono**, se cuecen sobre el brasero de carbón, con los ingredientes que van añadiendo los comensales. El secreto consiste en no poner demasiados a la vez, además el código de las buenas costumbres dice que hay que acabárselo. El personal del restaurante está siempre atento en caso de que se requiera su ayuda, y cuando se ha pedido **teppan-yaki** sofreirá a fuego vivo los ingredientes en la misma mesa, un espectáculo digno de verse.

PORTUGUÊS

A maioria das refeições é servida como um conjunto de pequenas doses individuais. No entanto, existem alguns pratos colectivos que são cozinhados na mesa. Os favoritos no Inverno, **nabe-mono**, são cozinhados lentamente num braseiro enquanto vão sendo adicionados os ingredientes. O segredo consiste em não cozinhar demasiados ingredientes ao mesmo tempo – mas mesmo assim, por delicadeza, não se deve deixar ficar nada, portanto verifique qual é a quantidade mínima servida. Os empregados estão sempre disponíveis para ajudar e, no caso do **teppan-yaki**, salteiam a comida à sua mesa. O **teppan** imbutido (chapa de ferro) também é utilizado para fritar o **okonomi-yaki.**

En Haute cuisine
F Haute cuisine
D Feine Küche
I Alta cucina
Es Cocina de lujo
P Alta cozinha

食通

ENGLISH

Kaiseki ryōri refers both to the ritual tea ceremony meal (懐石), named for the hot stone carried by Buddhists to ward off hunger pains, and to a formal dinner party of many consecutive courses (会席), usually served at ryō-tei and called after the venues where wandering poets used to perform. High class but informal cuisine can be enjoyed at a **kappō**, like a private dining room. Some take only one reservation a day, each dish decided in consultation with the chef. **Sushi** and **tempura** connoisseurs also take advice on the day's best finds, sitting at the counter to order piece by piece.

FRANÇAIS

Kaiseki ryōri fait référence à la cérémonie du thé (懐石), d'après la pierre chaude portée par les Bouddhistes pour tromper la faim ainsi qu'à un dîner formel comprenant divers plats successifs (会席), généralement servi à un **ryō-tei** et qui tire son nom des lieux où se produisaient les poètes itinérants. Une cuisine raffinée mais informelle est servie dans les **kappō**, sorte de salle à manger privée. Certaines n'acceptent qu'une réservation par jour, chaque plat étant sélectionné en concertation avec le chef. Les connaisseurs de **tempura** et de **sushi** suivent également les recommandations du chef en passant commande de chaque portion au comptoir.

DEUTSCH

Kaiseki ryōri bezeichnet sowohl die rituelle Teezeremonie (懐石), die nach dem heißen Stein benannt ist, den die Buddhisten am Körper trugen, um Hunger abzuwehren, als auch eine formelle Abendeinladung mit vielen aufeinander folgenden Gängen (会席), meist in einem **Ryō-tei**, nach den Stätten benannt, in denen früher wandemde Dichter auftraten. Feine, aber nicht so formelle Küche finden Sie in einem **Kappō**, ähnlich einem privaten Eßzimmer. Manche nehmen nur eine Reservierung pro Tag an, wobei jede Speise zusammen mit dem Küchenchef festgelegt wird. Kenner von **Sushi** und **Tempura** richten sich ebenfalls nach den besten Zutaten des Tages, sitzen an der Theke und bestellen jedes Sushi-Paar einzeln.

ITALIANO

Kaiseki ryōri si riferisce sia ai rituali del pasto con la cerimonia del tè (懐石) chiamato così per il nome della pietra calda che viene portata dai Buddisti per mandar via i morsi della fame) che ad una cena formale di molte portate consecutive (会席), di solito servita ad un **ryō-tei** e chiamata così secondo il nome dei luoghi dove poeti ambulanti si esibivano. Cucina di classe ma informale si può trovare ad un **kappō**, quasi una sala da pranzo privata. Alcune accettano solo una prenotazione al giorno ed ogni piatto viene deciso dopo aver consultato lo chef. I conoscitori di **sushi** e **tempura** accettano anche consigli sul piatto del giorno mentre siedono al bancone per ordinare pezzo per pezzo.

ESPAÑOL

Kaiseki ryōri significa tanto la comida que acompaña a la ceremonia del té (懐石), y cuyo nombre hace alusión a la piedra caliente que llevan los budistas para ahuyentar al fantasma del hambre, como una gran cena festiva compuesta por numerosos platos (会席), que se suele servir en el **ryō-tei** y cuya denominación se refiere a los puntos de reunión donde solían recitar los poetas itinerantes. En los **kappō** se puede disfrutar de una cocina excelente en un ambiente distendido, como si fuera un comedor casero. Algunos sólo aceptan una reserva al día, y cada plato se consulta con el jefe de cocina. Los entendidos en **sushi** y **tempura** siempre siguen las recomendaciones del día, sentados en la barra para ir degustando plato por plato.

PORTUGUÊS

Kaiseki ryōri designa a refeição da ritual do chá (懐石), que obteve o seu nome a partir da pedra quente usada pelos budistas para se protegerem contra as dores da fome. Também se refere a um jantar formal constituído por diversos pratos consecutivos (会席), normalmente servido num **ryō-tei**. Pode apreciar cozinha de qualidade elevada mas em ambiente informal num **kappō**, semelhante a uma sala de jantar privada. Alguns só aceitam uma reserva por dia e cada prato é escolhido após se ter consultado o chefe. Os apreciadores de **sushi** e de **tempura** também aproveitam as dicas sobre os melhores petiscos disponíveis e sentam-se ao balcão para fazer um pedido de cada vez.

- **En** Etiquette
- **F** Etiquette
- **D** Etikette
- **I** Etichetta
- **Es** Modales en la mesa
- **P** Etiqueta

作法

ENGLISH

Traditional Japanese food is ideally sized for chopsticks, but fish or large prawns must be pulled apart or bitten. Season to taste, dropping **wasabi** or spring onions into the dipping sauce or dribbling soy sauce onto grated radish. If sharing a central dish, take food to your plate or dip it before eating, and go back for more rather than take too much. Picking up bowls is fine, especially to catch drips or slurp soup, and chopsticks are handy to fish for titbits. With your companions' permission, start as soon as food is served – in any order, though **sashimi** and fresh **tempura** are best consumed first.

FRANÇAIS

L'assaisonnement est souvent complété par les convives. Du **wasabi** ou de la ciboule sont alors ajoutés à la sauce d'accompagnement, ou quelques gouttes de sauce de soja versées sur des radis râpés. Si vous partagez un plat, placez de la nourriture sur votre assiette, ou trempez-la dans de la sauce avant de la consommer, et n'empilez pas trop d'aliments sur votre assiette. Il est acceptable de soulever son bol, pour avaler une soupe par exemple, mais il vaut mieux utiliser ses baguettes pour saisir de petits morceaux. Avec l'agrément des autres convives, commencez à manger dès que vous êtes servi, sans respecter d'ordre de plats, bien qu'il vaille mieux commencer par le **sashimi** et le **tempura** frais.

DEUTSCH

Traditionelle japanische Speisen haben die ideale Größe für den Verzehr mit Eßstäbchen, Fisch und große Gamelen jedoch müssen Sie auseinanderreißen oder abbeißen. Würzen Sie nach Geschmack, streuen Sie **Wasabi** oder Frühlingszwiebeln in die Soße zum Tunken oder sprenkeln Sie Sojasoße auf geriebenen Rettich. Wenn Sie mit anderen von einem Gericht in der Mitte essen, nehmen Sie sich etwas davon auf Ihren Teller oder tunken Sie es zuerst in die Soße. Sie können Schüsseln durchaus zum Mund führen, etwa um Tropfen aufzufangen oder Suppe zu trinken. Eßstäbchen sind praktisch, um Köstlichkeiten einzeln herauszufischen. Wenn Ihre Begleiter es gestatten, fangen Sie mit dem Essen an, sobald es serviert wird.

ITALIANO

Il cibo tradizionale giapponese è di grandezza ideale per i bastoncini, ma pesce o gamberetti grossi devono essere strappati o morsi. Aggiungete condimento a piacere, versando **wasabi** o cipolline nella salsa in cui si inzuppa o schizzettando salsa di soia su ravanelli grattugiati. Se mangiate da un piatto centrale comune portate il vostro cibo sul piatto o inzuppatelo prima di mangiarlo e servitevi di nuovo dopo invece di prendere tutto insieme. Prendere in mano le ciotole é permesso – per non far cadere gocce o sorseggiare la minestra, ma i bastoncini sono proprio utili per raccogliere piccoli resti. Con il permesso dei vostri compagni cominciate appena il cibo è servito – in un qualsiasi ordine, anche se è sempre meglio mangiare prima **sashimi** e **tempura** freschi.

ESPAÑOL

La comida japonesa tiene el formato ideal para los palillos, aunque a veces hay que despedazar o morder el pescado o algunas gambas de gran tamaño. Sazonar al gusto, agregando **wasabi** o cebolletas a la salsa o rociando el rábano rallado con salsa de soja. Si está compartiendo una comida a rancho con los demás comensales, llévese su parte al plato o úntela en la salsa antes de comerla. Es mejor repetir que servirse demasiado. No está mal visto levantar el bol, para evitar mancharse la ropa o para sorber la sopa; los palillos resultan muy prácticos para pescar los deliciosos trocitos que queden. Puede empezar en cuanto traen la comida, no importa el orden, aunque se recomienda iniciar el ágape con el **sashimi** y el **tempura** recién hecho.

PORTUGUÊS

Tempere a gosto, passando o **wasabi** ou o cebolinho no molho, ou espalhando molho de soja sobre o rabanete ralado. Caso tenha optado por partilhar um prato central, ponha a comida no seu prato ou passe-a pelo molho antes de comer e sirva-se de novo, em vez de tirar uma grande quantidade de uma só vez. Não há problema em pegar nas taças para sorver a sopa ou apanhar as gotas - embora os pauzinhos sejam muito práticos para apanhar bocados pequenos. Com a permissão dos seus companheiros, comece a comer mal a comida seja servida – pode experimentar cada prato segundo qualquer ordem, embora seja melhor começar pelo **sashimi** e pela **tempura** fresca.

En Philosophy
F Philosophie
D Philosophie
I Filosofia
Es Filosofía
P A filosofia

哲学

ENGLISH

In the Japanese ethos, to appreciate good food is to celebrate the blessings of the gods. Fish and vegetables are enjoyed in season, their flavours respected by minimal cooking or heightened by natural taste enhancers such as kelp, while salt and sweet must be perfectly balanced. This is all in the quest for **umami** – the essential taste and feel of any food. With formal cuisine, presentation matters even more than flavour, to delight the eye and inspire the appetite. Garnishes emphasize the season and ingredients like citrus peel may be added simply for the aroma which gathers beneath the lid of a bowl.

FRANÇAIS

Dans la philosophie japonaise, en appréciant une bonne nourriture, on porte hommage aux dieux. Poissons et légumes de la saison sont appréciés, et leurs saveurs sont préservées grâce à un minimum de cuisson ou sont mises en relief, par exemple, avec du varech. Les saveurs sucrées et salées parfaitement équilibrées permettent aussi d'atteindre l'umami, goût et consistance essentiels de toute nourriture. Dans une cuisine formelle, la présentation est encore plus importante que le goût pour flatter l'œil et stimuler l'appétit. Les garnitures se font écho de la saison et un zeste de citron peut par exemple être ajouté pour l'arôme qu'il dégagera au soulever du couvercle.

DEUTSCH

In Japan feiert man mit dem Genuß von gutem Essen den Segen der Götter. Fisch und Gemüse werden in der Saison zubereitet, ihr Geschmack wird durch einen möglichst einfachen Kochvorgang erhalten oder durch natürliche Geschmacksverstärker wie Kelpalge betont. Salz und Süße sowie Geschmack und Konsistenz müssen perfekt ausbalanciert sein, um **Umami** zu erhalten, d. h. dem Wesen der Speise perfekt zu entsprechen. Bei formeller Küche ist die Darbietung noch wichtiger als der Geschmack, um das Auge zu erfreuen und den Appetit anzuregen. Garnierungen beziehen sich auf die Jahreszeit. Zutaten wie Zitronenschale werden oft nur deswegen hinzugefügt, weil sie ein angenehmes Aroma in der zugedeckten Schüssel erzeugen.

ITALIANO

Nell'etica giapponese apprezzare il cibo buono è celebrare le benedizioni degli dei. Il pesce e le verdure sono godute nelle loro stagioni, i loro sapori sono rispettati con cottura minima o rinforzati con aromi naturali quali l'alga marina, mentre il salato ed il dolce devono essere bilanciati perfettamente al fine di raggiungere l'**umami** – il sapore e la consistenza di qualsiasi cibo allo stato puro. Per la cucina formale, al fine di appagare l'occhio e ispirare l'appetito, la presentazione è di importanza ancora maggiore del sapore. Le guarnizioni mettono in rilievo le stagioni e ingredienti come la scorza di agrumi possono essere aggiunti soltanto perché arricchiscono l'aroma che si crea sotto il tappo di una ciotola.

ESPAÑOL

En la cultura japonesa, saber apreciar la buena comida es como celebrar la bendición de los dioses. Se consume pescado y verdura del tiempo, respetando sus sabores propios elaborándolos lo mínimo posible o resaltando su sabor con potenciadores naturales como las algas marinas; el objetivo es conseguir una expresión perfecta de sabores y consistencias, aspirando a lograr el **umami**, el aroma y tacto esencial de todo alimento. En la gastronomía de altos vuelos, la presentación es incluso más importante que el sabor, para deleitar la vista y despertar el apetito. Los aderezos representan la estación del año, y a veces se añaden ingredientes como la piel de un cítrico simplemente por recrearse en el aroma que se forma bajo la tapa del cuenco.

PORTUGUÊS

Para a cultura japonesa, apreciar boa comida é celebrar as bençãos dos deuses. O peixe e os vegetais são apreciados na sua época própria e o seu gosto natural é preservado, graças a uma confecção reduzida, ou realçado através da utilização de produtos naturais, como as algas. O doce e o salgado devem encontrar-se em perfeito equilíbrio. Tudo isto para se alcançar o **umami** – o gosto essencial de cada alimento. Na cozinha formal, o aspecto tem ainda mais importância do que o sabor, para dar prazer ao olhar e inspirar o apetite. As guarnições salientam a época e produtos como a casca de citrinos podem ser adicionados apenas por causa do aroma que se forma sob a tampa da taça.

83

En Diet
F Régime alimentaire
D Ernährung
I Dieta
Es Dieta
P Dieta

健康

ENGLISH

The traditional healthy diet is based on rice, fish and vegetables but **shōjin ryōri**, the vegan cuisine of Buddhism, is still served as **kaiseki ryōri** and its legacy in daily cuisine is the use of vegetarian jellies and oils, and protein-rich soy bean products like **miso**, soy sauce and **tōfu**. Pork, fowl and game pre-date Buddhism, and 19th century traders revived the eating of beef, but a meat and dairy-free diet is still easy to achieve. Fish stock is a basic ingredient, however, and gluten balls are used for decoration, so inform staff of what you cannot eat.

FRANÇAIS

L'alimentation traditionnelle, très saine, est à base de riz, de poisson et de légumes, mais **shōjin ryōri**, cuisine végétalienne bouddhiste, est toujours servie en tant que **kaiseki ryōri**. Son influence dans la cuisine quotidienne apparaît surtout dans les huiles et gelées végétariennes et dans les produits à base de graines de soja, très riches en protéines, tels que le **miso**, la sauce de soja et le **tōfu**. La consommation de porc, de volaille et de gibier remonte à avant le Bouddhisme et les négociants du 19ième siècle remirent le bœuf à la mode. Cependant, il est toujours facile de manger sans viande ni produits laitiers. Le bouillon de poisson est un ingrédient de base et des boulettes de gluten sont souvent utilisées comme décoration; précisez donc si vous voulez les éviter.

DEUTSCH

Die herkömmliche, gesunde Ernährung besteht aus Reis, Fisch und Gemüse, doch wird **Shōjin ryōri**, die veganische Küche des Buddhismus, immer noch serviert und ist in der alltäglichen Küche an der Verwendung von vegetarischen Geliermitteln und Ölen sowie eiweißreichen Sojabohnenprodukten wie **Miso**, Sojasoße und **Tōfu** zu erkennen. Schweinefleisch, Geflügel und Wild gehen auf vorbuddhistische Zeiten zurück, und die Händler des 19. Jh. führten Rindfleischgerichte wieder ein, doch ist es immer noch einfach, sich ohne Fleisch und Milchprodukte zu ernähren. Fischfond ist eine wichtige Zutat und Glutenbällchen werden in Garnierungen verwendet. Geben Sie deshalb dem Kellner immer an, welche Lebensmittel Sie meiden.

ITALIANO

La sana dieta tradizionale si basa su riso, pesce e verdura, ma la **shōjin ryōri** – la cucina vegana del buddhismo – è ancora servita come **kaiseki ryōri** e la sua influenza sulla cucina giornaliera si nota nell'uso di gelatine, oli vegetariani e prodotti ricchi di proteine provenienti dal seme di soia come il **miso**, la salsa di soia ed il **tōfu**. Il maiale, il pollame e la cacciagione sono precedenti al Buddhismo e i mercanti del diciannovesimo secolo recuperarono l'uso del manzo, ma è ancora facile ottenere una dieta priva di carne e di prodotti caseari. In ogni caso il brodo di pesce è un ingrediente di base e le polpette di glutine sono molto usate per la decorazione, quindi è necessario informare o staff se non potete mangiare qualcosa.

ESPAÑOL

La dieta sana y tradicional se basa en arroz, pescado y verduras. La cocina vegetariana budista, **shōjin ryōri**, todavía se sirve como **kaiseki ryōri**. Su legado para la cocina cotidiana es el uso de jaleas y aceites vegetales, y los productos derivados de la soja ricos en proteínas, como el **miso**, la salsa de soja y el **tōfu**. El cerdo, las aves y la caza son anteriores al budismo; los comerciantes del siglo XIX reintrodujeron el consumo del vacuno, aunque no es problema conseguir una dieta libre de carnes y lácteos. El caldo de pescado es un ingrediente básico, y para adornar los platos se utilizan bolas de gluten, por lo cual si no puede comer estos alimentos tiene que informar al personal del restaurante.

PORTUGUÊS

A dieta saudável tradicional tem como base o arroz, o peixe e os vegetais, mas a **shōjin ryōri**, a cozinha vegetariana budista, ainda é servida como **kaiseki ryōri**. O seu legado na cozinha diária consiste na utilização frequente de gelatinas e óleos vegetais e de produtos derivados da soja, ricos em proteínas, como o **miso**, o molho de soja e o **tōfu**. O porco, as aves de capoeira e a caça são ingredientes anteriores ao budismo e os comerciantes do século XIX fizeram reviver a tradição de comer carne de vaca, mas é fácil obter uma dieta sem carne e produtos lacticínios. No entanto, o caldo de peixe é um ingrediente básico e as bolas de glúten são utilizadas na decoração, por isso é melhor informar os empregados sobre aquilo que não pode comer.

- **En** Regional influences
- **F** Influences régionales
- **D** Regionale Einflüsse
- **I** Influenze regionali
- **Es** Influencias regionales
- **P** Influências regionais

歴史

ENGLISH

Local specialities vary from salmon hotpot in Hokkaido to the pork stews of Kyushu. Around Tokyo, **kantō**-style cooking uses dark soy sauce, whereas the rival **kansai**-style from Osaka and Kyoto emphasizes subtle natural flavours and transparent sauces. Overseas influences have also been readily absorbed, such as **rāmen**, **chāhan** and **gyōza** from China, and **tempura** was originally Portuguese. Now **yaki-niku** restaurants serve Korean barbecue-style beef, and **famirī resutoran** offer Japanized burgers and spaghetti, while top chefs pride themselves on developing rich new fusion cuisines.

FRANÇAIS

Les spécialités locales vont de la matelote de saumon de Hokkaido aux ragoûts de porc de Kyushu. Dans la région de Tokyo, les plats de style **kantō** sont assaisonnés de sauce de soja brune qui tranche avec le style **kansai** d'Osaka et de Kyoto tout en subtiles saveurs naturelles et en sauces limpides. Les influences étrangères ont été absorbées par la cuisine locale, **rāmen**, **chāhan** et **gyōza** provenant de Chine et **tempura** étant d'origine portugaise. De nos jours, les restaurants **yaki-niku** offrent du bœuf grillé à la mode coréenne et les **famirī resutoran** servent des hamburgers et des spaghettis à la japonaise. Les grands chefs, eux, sont fiers de créer de nouvelles saveurs en faisant fusionner différentes influences culinaires.

DEUTSCH

Lokale Spezialitäten sind vielfältig, von Lachstopf in Hokkaido zu den Schweinefleischeintöpfen aus Kyushu. Um Tokyo wird im **Kantō**-Stil gekocht, d.h. mit dunkler Sojasoße, während beim **Kansai**-Stil in Osaka und Kyoto die zarten, natürlichen Aromen und durchsichtige Soßen dominieren. Auch ausländische Einflüsse wurden aufgenommen, wie etwa **Rāmen**, **Chāhan** und **Gyōza** aus China. **Tempura** war ursprünglich portugiesisch. Heute servieren **Yaki-niku** Restaurants koreanisch gegrilltes Rindfleisch und **Famirī resutoran** bieten japanisierte Hamburger und Spaghetti an. Die besten Küchenchefs setzen ihren Stolz darauf, neue Stile aus einer Fusion der bestehenden zu entwickeln.

ITALIANO

Le specialità locali variano dallo stufato di salmone a Hokkaido allo spezzatino di maiale a Kyushu. La cucina **kantō**, lo stile della zona intorno a Tokyo, usa salsa di soia scura mentre quella rivale, la **kansai**, tipica della zona di Osaka e Kyoto, mette in rilievo i delicati sapori naturali e salse trasparenti. Influenze straniere sono anche state assorbite velocemente, per esempio l'uso del **rāmen**, del **chāhan** e del **gyōza** dalla Cina, ed il **tempura** era originariamente portoghese. Adesso i ristoranti **yaki-niku** servono manzo al barbecue coreano e i ristoranti **famirī resutoran** offrono hamburger e spaghetti un po' alla giapponese, mentre gli chef migliori si vantano di sviluppare nuovi tipi di cucina derivati dalla fusione con altre tradizioni.

ESPAÑOL

Las especialidades locales varían desde el salmón estofado de Hokkaido hasta los cocidos de cerdo de Kyushu. En Tokyo y cercanías, la cocina **kantō** utiliza salsa negra de soja, mientras que la cocina rival **kansai**, originaria de Osaka y Kyoto, enfatiza los sutiles sabores naturales y prefiere salsas transparentes. La gastronomía japonesa ha absorbido también las costumbres de otros países y culturas, adoptando por ejemplo el **rāmen**, **chāhan** y **gyōza** de China; el **tempura**, por otro lado, tiene sus raíces en la cocina portuguesa. Actualmente, los restaurantes **yaki-niku** sirven ternera asada al estilo coreano, y los **famirī resutoran** ofrecen versiones japonesas de hamburguesas y espaguetis.

PORTUGUÊS

As especialidades locais vão desde o estufado de salmão em Hokkaido aos guisados de porco em Kyushu. Nos arredores de Tóquio, a cozinha **kantō** , típica da região, utiliza molho de soja escuro, enquanto a **kansai**, cozinha rival de Osaka e de Kyoto, prefere sabores mais subtis e naturais e molhos transparentes. Foram absorvidas facilmente influências estrangeiras, como o **rāmen**, o **chāhan** e o **gyōza** da China, e a **tempura** originalmente era um prato português. Hoje em dia, os restaurantes **yaki-niku** servem carne de vaca grelhada no espeto à coreana e os **famirī resutoran** oferecem hamburgers e esparguete à japonesa, enquanto chefes conceituados se orgulham de desenvolver cozinhas ricas através da fusão de diversas tradições.

En Chopsticks
F Les baguettes
D Eßstäbchen
I Bastoncini
Es Palillos
P Pauzinhos

箸

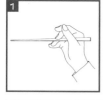

会 話
KAIWA

- **En** Useful phrases
- **F** Phrases utiles
- **D** Nützliche Redewendungen
- **I** Expresiones útiles
- **Es** Frases utiles
- **P** Frases úteis

En Useful phrases
F Phrases utiles
D Nützliche Redewendungen
I Frasi utili
Es Expresiones útiles
P Frases úteis

♪ Oishii **izaka-ya / soba-ya** o gozonji desu ka?　　おいしい居酒屋/そば屋をご存じですか？

En Can you recommend a good **izaka-ya / soba-ya**?

F Pouvez-vous me recommander un bon **izaka-ya / soba-ya** ?

D Können Sie ein gutes **Izaka-ya / Soba-ya** empfehlen?

I Mi può consigliare un buon **izaka-ya / soba-ya**?

Es ¿Me puede recomendar un buen **izaka-ya / soba-ya**?

P Pode recomendar-me um bom **izaka-ya / soba-ya**?

♪ San(3)-nin suwaremasu ka?　　3人座れますか？

En Can you seat three people?

F Avez-vous de la place pour trois personnes ?

D Haben Sie noch Platz für drei Personen?

I C'è posto per tre?

Es ¿Hay sitio para tres personas?

P Há lugar para três pessoas?

♪ Dorekurai machimasu ka?　どれくらい待ちますか？

🇬🇧 How long is the wait?
🇫🇷 Combien de temps faudra-t-il attendre ?
🇩🇪 Wie lange muß man warten?
🇮🇹 Quanto c'è da aspettare?
🇪🇸 ¿Cuánto tenemos que esperar?
🇵🇹 Quanto tempo vai demorar?

♪ Hachi(8)-ji ni san(3)-nin yoyaku dekimasu ka?　8時に3人予約できますか？

🇬🇧 Can I make a reservation for three people at 8pm?
🇫🇷 Je voudrais réserver pour trois personnes à 8 heures.
🇩🇪 Können Sie mir einen Tisch für drei Personen für 8 Uhr reservieren?
🇮🇹 Posso prenotare per tre persone per le otto di sera?
🇪🇸 ¿Puedo hacer una reserva para tres personas para las 8 de la noche?
🇵🇹 É possível fazer uma reserva para três pessoas, para as 8 horas?

♪ Kyō no o-susume wa nan desu ka?　今日のおすすめは何ですか？

🇬🇧 What do you recommend today?
🇫🇷 Quelles sont les spécialités du jour ?
🇩🇪 Was können Sie heute empfehlen?
🇮🇹 Che cosa ci consiglia oggi?
🇪🇸 ¿Qué nos recomienda hoy?
🇵🇹 O que é que recomenda para hoje?

♪ Kore wa nan desu ka?　これは何ですか？

🇬🇧 What is this?
🇫🇷 Qu'est-ce que c'est ?
🇩🇪 Was ist das?
🇮🇹 Questo che cosa è?
🇪🇸 ¿Qué es ésto?
🇵🇹 O que é isto?

♪ Rōma-ji de kaite itadakemasu ka?　ローマ字で書いていただけますか？

🇬🇧 Please write this in the roman alphabet.

🇫🇷 Pourriez-vous écrire cela en caractères romains ?

🇩🇪 Bitte schreiben Sie das in römischem Alphabet auf.

🇮🇹 Lo può riscrivere usando l'alfabeto romano per favore?

🇪🇸 Hágame el favor de escribir ésto en alfabeto romano.

🇵🇹 Por favor, pode escrever isso em caracteres ocidentais?

♪ Kore niwa nani ga tsuite kimasu ka?　これには何が付いてきますか？

🇬🇧 What comes with this meal?

🇫🇷 En quoi consiste exactement ce plat ?

🇩🇪 Was gehört zu dieser Mahlzeit?

🇮🇹 Questo pasto che cosa comprende?

🇪🇸 ¿Con qué viene acompañado este plato?

🇵🇹 O que é que acompanha este prato?

♪ Kore wa dorekurai no ryō desu ka?　これはどれくらいの量ですか？

🇬🇧 How much food is this?

🇫🇷 Pourriez-vous me donner une idée des quantités servies ?

🇩🇪 Wieviel Essen ist das?

🇮🇹 Questo quanto cibo è?

🇪🇸 ¿Qué cantidad de comida es?

🇵🇹 Qual é a quantidade de comida?

♪ Are o kudasai　あれを下さい。

🇬🇧 I want one like that, please.

🇫🇷 J'en voudrais un comme cela, s'il vous plaît.

🇩🇪 Ich möchte so eines bitte.

🇮🇹 Ne vorrei uno così, per favore.

🇪🇸 Tráigame uno de esos, por favor.

🇵🇹 Queria um igual àquele, se faz favor.

♪ O-shokuji / o-nomi-mono wa nani ni nasaimasu ka?　お食事/お飲物 は何になさいますか？

🇬🇧 What would you like to **eat** / **drink**? *(waitress)*
🇫🇷 Que désirez-vous **manger** / **boire** ? *(serveuse)*
🇩🇪 Was möchten Sie **essen** / **trinken**? *(Kellnerin)*
🇮🇹 Che cosa desiderano da **mangiare** / **bere**? *(cameriera)*
🇪🇸 ¿Qué desea **comer** / **beber**? *(camarera)*
🇵🇹 O que quer **comer** / **beber**? *(empregado)*

♪ Ebi no tempura / bīru wa arimasu ka?　海老の天ぷら/ビール はありますか？

🇬🇧 Do you have **prawn tempura** / **beer**?
🇫🇷 Est-ce que vous avez des **beignets de crevettes** / de la **bière** ?
🇩🇪 Haben Sie **Garnelen-Tempura** / **Bier**?
🇮🇹 Avete **gamberetti tempura** / **birra**?
🇪🇸 ¿Hay **tempura de langostino** / **cerveza**?
🇵🇹 Tem **tempura de gambas** / **cerveja**?

♪ Ebi no tempura / bīru / kore o kudasai.　海老の天ぷら/ビール/これを下さい。

🇬🇧 I'd like **prawn tempura** / **beer** / **this one**, please.
🇫🇷 Je voudrais des **beignets de crevettes** / de la **bière** / **ceci**, s'il vous plaît.
🇩🇪 Ich hätte gerne **Garnelen-Tempura** / **Bier** / **dies** bitte.
🇮🇹 Vorrei **gamberetti tempura** / **birra** / **questo** per favore.
🇪🇸 ¿Me traería **tempura de langostino** / **cerveza** / **esto**, por favor?
🇵🇹 Queria **tempura de gambas** / **cerveja** / **isto** se faz favor.

♪ Sumimasen, sore wa gozaimasen...　すみません、それはございません…

🇬🇧 Sorry, we don't have that. *(waitress)*
🇫🇷 Je suis désolée, nous n'avons pas cela. *(serveuse)*
🇩🇪 Das haben wir leider nicht. *(Kellnerin)*
🇮🇹 Mi dispiace, non lo abbiamo. *(cameriera)*
🇪🇸 Lo siento, no hay. *(camarera)*
🇵🇹 Desculpe, mas não temos. *(empregado)*

♪ Gyū-niku / kai / nattsu wa tabemasen.   牛肉/貝類/ナッツ類 は食べません。

En I don't eat **beef** / **shellfish** / **nuts**.

Fr Je ne mange pas de **bœuf** / de **crustacés** / de **noix, noisettes,** etc.

De Ich esse kein **Rindfleisch** / keine **Muscheln** / keine **Nüsse**.

It Non mangio **manzo** / **molluschi** / **noci**.

Es No como **carne de vaca** / **mariscos** / **nueces**.

Pt Não como **carne de vaca** / **crustáceos** / **nozes, amendoins,** etc.

♪ Watashi wa bejitarian desu.   私はベジタリアンです。

En I am vegetarian / vegan.

Fr Je suis végétarien / végétalien.

De Ich bin Vegetarier / Veganer.

It Sono vegetariano / vegano.

Es Soy vegetariano / vegano.

Pt Sou vegetariano.

♪ Sumimasen!   すみません!

En Excuse me! *(for attention)*

Fr S'il vous plaît ! *(pour attirer l'attention)*

De Entschuldigen Sie bitte! *(um Aufmerksamkeit bitten)*

It Scusi! *(per richiamare l'attenzione)*

Es ¡Oiga! *(para llamar la atención)*

Pt Desculpe... / Por favor... *(para chamar a atenção)*

♪ O-tsukuri shite yoroshii desu ka?   お作りしてよろしいですか?

En Do you mind me doing it for you? *(waitress)*

Fr Puis-je vous aider ? *(serveuse)*

De Möchten Sie, daß ich das für Sie tue? *(Kellnerin)*

It Glielo posso fare io? *(cameriera)*

Es ¿Me permite que le ayude? *(camarera)*

Pt Não prefere que seja eu a fazer isso? *(empregado)*

♪ Itadakimasu!　いただきます！

🇬🇧 *(thanks before food)*

🇫🇷 *(mot de remerciement prononcés en début de repas)*

🇩🇪 *(Dank vor dem Essen)*

🇮🇹 *(ringraziamento a chi porta il cibo o agli dei)*

🇪🇸 *(gracias antes de empezar a comer)*

🇵🇹 *(agradecimentos, antes da comida)*

♪ Gochisō sama deshita　ごちそう様でした。

🇬🇧 I'm full! That was delicious! *(to end meal)*

🇫🇷 J'ai très bien mangé. C'était délicieux! *(à la fin du repas)*

🇩🇪 Ich bin satt! Das war köstlich! *(am Ende der Mahlzeit)*

🇮🇹 Sono pieno! Era un pasto delizioso. *(alla fine del pasto)*

🇪🇸 Estoy satisfecho. ¡Estaba riquísimo! *(al terminar la comida)*

🇵🇹 Estou satisfeito! Estava delicioso! *(para terminar a refeição)*

♪ Tabako o sutte iidesu ka?　タバコを吸っていいですか？

🇬🇧 May I smoke?

🇫🇷 Est-ce que cela vous dérange si je fume ?

🇩🇪 Darf ich rauchen?

🇮🇹 Posso fumare?

🇪🇸 ¿Puedo fumar?

🇵🇹 Posso fumar?

♪ O-kanjō o onegai shimasu.　お勘定をお願いします。

🇬🇧 May I have the bill, please?

🇫🇷 L'addition, s'il vous plaît.

🇩🇪 Kann ich bitte die Rechnung haben?

🇮🇹 Mi può portare il conto per favore?

🇪🇸 ¿Me trae la cuenta, por favor?

🇵🇹 A conta, por favor.

En Reading Japanese

F Caractères japonais

D Japanisch lesen

I Leggere il giapponese

Es Caracteres japonesas

P Ler japonês

Some Japanese words can be written two different ways

Certains mots japonais ont deux graphies différentes

Einige japanische Wörter können auf zwei Arten geschrieben werden

Alcune parole giapponesi possono essere scritte in due modi diversi

Algunas expresiones japonesas se pueden escribir de dos maneres

Algumas palavras japonêsas podem se escrever de duas maneiras

JAPANESE		RŌMA-JI
定食	ていしょく	teishoku
	セット	setto
	ランチ	ranchi
今日のお薦め	今日のおすすめ	kyō no o-susume
一品料理	いっぴんりょうり	ippin ryōri
前菜	ぜんさい	zensai
和え物	あえもの	ae-mono
酢の物	すのもの	suno-mono
焼き物	やきもの	yaki-mono
揚げ物	あげもの	age-mono
煮物	にもの	ni-mono
鍋物	なべもの	nabe-mono
丼物	どんぶりもの	domburi-mono

読む

メニューと言葉
MENU TO KOTOBA

JAPANESE	ENGLISH	FRANÇAIS
aji	horse mackerel, scad	chinchard, saurel
akagai	ark shell	arche de Noé
ama-ebi	sweet prawn	crevette nordique
anago	conger eel	congre
chirashi-zushi	bowl of **sushi** (lit. scattered **sushi**)	bol de **sushi** (lit. **sushi** éparpillé)
ebi	prawn	crevette
futo-maki	thick roll w. many ingredients	gros rouleau aux nombreux ingrédients
hamachi	young yellowtail, amberjack	sériole
hirame	false halibut, brill	fausse limande, barbue
hotategai	scallop	coquille St-Jacques
ika	squid	encornet, seiche
ikura	salmon roe	œufs de saumon
inari-zushi	vinegared rice in fried **tōfu** bags (lit. fox's **sushi**)	**tōfu** farci de riz au vinaigre (lit. **sushi** du renard)

DEUTSCH	ITALIANO	ESPAÑOL	PORTUGUÊS
Bastardmakrele, Holzmakrele	suro, sugarello	jurel	cavala, chicharro
Archenmuschel	arca, la comune arca di noè	arca de Noé (almeja)	concha de arca amêijoa
Nordmeergarnele	pandalo, code di granchio	camarón dulce	camarão
Congeraal	gronco, anguilla di mare	congrio	enguia do mar
Sushi im Schüsselchen (wörtl. verstreutes **Sushi**)	ciotola di **sushi** (lett. **sushi** sparpagliato)	bol de **sushi** (lit. **sushi** desparramado)	taça de **sushi** (lit. **sushi** espalhado)
Königsgarnele, Riesengarnele	gamberetto	langostino	gamba
Dicke Rolle m. vielen Zutaten	involto con molti ingredienti	rollo grueso con muchos ingredientes	crepe espesso c/ muitos ingredientes
Jap. Seriola	ricciola, leccia	sorel	linguadinho
Jap. Heilbutt, Brill, Steinbutt	nei nostri mari il rombo	remol, rodaballo	solha
Pilgermuschel, Jakobsmuschel	pettine	vieira	vieira
Kalmar	calamaro, totano	calamar, sepia	lula
Lachsrogen	uova di salmone	huevas de salmón	ovas de salmão
marinierter Reis in gebrat. **Tōfu**-taschen (wörtl. Fuchs-**Sushi**)	**tōfu** fritto ripieno di riso all'aceto (lett. **sushi** delle volpi)	arroz con vinagre en bolsitas de **tōfu** fritas	arroz em saquinhos de **tōfu** frito (lit. **sushi** de raposa)

JAPANESE	ENGLISH	FRANÇAIS
kappa-maki	cucumber roll (lit. goblin roll)	rouleau au concombre (lit. rouleau du farfadet)
maguro	tuna	thon
mirugai	gaper, horse clam	mye
saba	mackerel	maquereau
sake, shake	salmon	saumon
suzuki	sea bass	loup de mer
tako	octopus	poulpe
tamago-yaki	omelette	omelette
tekka-maki	tuna roll (lit. gamblers' roll)	rouleau de thon (lit. rouleau du joueur)
torigai	cockle	coques
toro	fatty tuna belly	morceau gras du thon
unagi	freshwater eel	anguille d'eau douce
uni	sea urchin roe	œufs d'oursin

DEUTSCH	ITALIANO	ESPAÑOL	PORTUGUÊS
Gurkenrolle (wörtl. Geisterrolle)	involtino di cetriolo (lett. involtino del folletto)	rollito de pepino (lit. rollito del duende)	rolhino de pepino (lit. rolhino "Gnomo")
Tunfisch	tonno	atún	atum
Sandklaffmuschel	mollusco del cavallo	tipo de almeja	ameijola
Makrele	sgombro, macarello	caballa	cavala, cavalinha
Lachs	salmone	salmón	salmão
Zackenbarsch, Seewolf	persico, spigola, cernia	lubina grande	robalo
Polyp, Oktopus	polipo	pulpo	polvo
Omelett	omelette	tortilla de huevo	omeleta
Tunfischrolle (wörtl. Spielerrolle)	involtino di tonno (lett. involtino del giocatore)	rollito de atún (lit. rollito del jugador)	volinho de atum (lit. rolinho de jogador)
Herzmuschel	cardio, arsella	berberecho	berbigão
fetter Tunfischbauch	pancia di tonno - parte grassa	ventresca de atún	barriga de atum gordo
Süßwasseraal	anguilla	anguila de agua dulce	enguia de água doce
Seeigelrogen	uova di riccio di mare	huevas de erizo de mar	ovas de ouriço do mar

JAPANESE	ENGLISH	FRANÇAIS
ebi	prawn	crevette
ika	squid	encornet, seiche
kabocha	pumpkin	potiron
kaki-age	mixed fritter of chopped seafood + veg	friture mixte de fruits de mer + légumes
kisu	sillago, Japanese whiting	merlan japonais
mai-take	hen-of-the-woods fungus	champignon brun très recherché
nasu	aubergine	aubergine
renkon	lotus root	racine de lotus
shii-take	brown mushroom	champignon brun
shishitō	small green pepper, capsicum	petit poivron vert
shiso	beefsteak plant	herbe aromatique, sorte de menthe poivrée
shungiku	chrysanthemum	chrysanthème
tama-negi	onion	oignon

DEUTSCH	ITALIANO	ESPAÑOL	PORTUGUÊS
Königsgarnele, Riesengarnele	gamberetto	langostino	gamba
Kalmar	calamaro, totano	calamar, sepia	lula
Kürbis	zucca	calabaza	abóbora-menina
gemischte Meeresfrüchte + Gemüse, frittiert	fritto misto di pesce + verdura a pezzetti	buñuelo de marisco + verdura picados	mistura frita de marisco + legumes
Wittling	merlango, muggine	pescadilla	pescada japonesa
Maitake Pilz	fungo autunnale coltivabile maitakè (grifola frondosa)	mai-take (deliciosa seta otoñal de color pardo)	cogumelo "dancante", grande e muito apreciado
Aubergine	melanzana	berenjena	beringela
Lotuswurzel	fusto sotterraneo del loto indiano	raíz de loto	raiz de lótus
Shitake Pilz	fungo marrone coltivabile shitakè (lentinus edodes)	seta de color pardo	cogumelo castanho
kl. grüner Paprika	peperone verde	pimiento verde pequeño	pimentão verde pequeno
Shiso Perilla	menta perilla, pepolino	planta aromática parecida a la menta	ingrediente tipo hortelã
Chrysantheme	crisantemo	crisantemo	crisântemo
Zwiebel	cipolla	cebolla	cebola

JAPANESE	ENGLISH	FRANÇAIS
aji furai	deep-fried, breaded horse mackerel	chinchard pané et frit
chikin-katsu	deep-fried, breaded chicken breast / thigh	blanc / cuisse de poulet pané et frit
ebi furai	deep-fried, breaded prawn	crevettes panées et frites
hire-katsu	deep-fried, breaded fillet of pork	filet de porc pané et frit
kaki furai	deep-fried, breaded oyster	huîtres panées et frites
kani-kurīmu -korokke	croquette of white sauce + crab	croquette de crabe à la sauce blanche
korokke	croquette of onion + potato + pork / fish	croquette d'oignon + pomme de terre + porc / poisson
kushi-age	deep-fried, skewered meat / fish / veg	brochette de viande / poisson / légumes frits
kushi-katsu	deep-fried, skewered pork + spring onion	brochette de porc + ciboules frites
menchi-katsu	deep-fried, breaded patty of meat + onion	petit pâté frit à la viande + oignons
mikkusu furai	assortment of deep-fried meat / fish / veg	assortiment de viande / poisson / légumes frits
ton-katsu	deep-fried, breaded pork cutlet	côtelette de porc panée et frite
ton-katsu sōsu	thick sweet brown sauce	sauce brune sucrée épaisse

豚かつ

DEUTSCH	ITALIANO	ESPAÑOL	PORTUGUÊS
frittierte, panierte Holzmakrele	suro impanato e fritto	jurel rebozado y frito	chicharro panados
frittierte, panierte Hühnerbrust/-keule	petto / anca di pollo impanato e fritto	pechuga / muslo de pollo, rebozados y fritos	peito / coxa de galinha panado
frittierte, panierte Garnele	gamberetto impanato e fritto	langostino rebozado y frito	gamba panada
frittiertes, paniertes Schweinefilet	filetto di maiale impanato e fritto	filete de cerdo rebozado y frito	fêvera de porco panada
frittierte, panierte Auster	ostrica impanata e fritta	ostra rebozada y frita	ostra panada
Krebskrokette m. weißer Soße	crocchetta di salsa bianca + granchio	croqueta con salsa blanca + cangrejo	croquete de caranguejo + molho branco
Krokette aus Zwiebel + Kartoffel + Schweinefl. / Fisch	crocchetta di cipolla + patata + maiale / pesce	croqueta de cebolla + patata + carne de cerdo / mariscos	croquete de cebola + batata + porco / peixe
Fleisch / Fisch / Gemüse am Spieß, frittiert	spiedino fritto di carne / pesce / verdura	brochetas fritas de carne / marisco / verduras	espetadas fritas de carne / peixe / legumes
Schweinefl. + Frühlingszwiebel am Spieß frittiert	spiedinofritto di maiale + cipolline	brochetas de carne de cerdo + cebolleta, fritas	espetadas fritas de porco + cebolinho
Fleischlaibchen paniert, frittiert	polpetta di carne + cipolla impanata e fritta	hamburguesa de carne + cebolla, rebozada y frita	pastel panado de carne + cebola
frittierte Mischung aus Fleisch / Fisch / Gemüse	fritto misto di carne / pesce / verdura	selección de carnes / mariscos / verduras fritas	sortido frito de carne / peixe / legumes
frittierte, paniertes Schweinskotelett	cotoletta di maiale impanata e fritta	costilla de cerdo rebozada y frita	costeleta de porco panada
dicke, süße, braune Soße	salsa scura dolce e densa	salsa dulce espesa de color marrón	molho espesso castanho e doce

YAKI-TORI MENU

JAPANESE	ENGLISH	FRANÇAIS
gatsu	intestines	intestins
gin-nan	gingko nut	noix de gingko
hatsu	heart	cœur
nan-kotsu	cartilage	cartilage
rebā	liver	foie
shiro	tripe	tripes
suna-gimo	gizzard	gésier
tan	tongue	langue
teba-saki	wingtip	extrémité de l'aile
tori-kawa	chicken skin	peau de poulet
tsukune	meatballs	boulettes de viande
uzura no tamago	quail egg	œuf de caille
wasabi-yaki	chicken pieces with **wasabi**	morceaux de poulet avec **wasabi**

DEUTSCH	ITALIANO	ESPAÑOL	PORTUGUÊS
Gedärme	interiora	intestinos	intestinos
Gingko-Nuß	noce ginkgo	nuez de gingko	noz de gincgo
Herz	cuore	corazón	coração
Knorpel	cartilagine	cartílago	cartilagem
Leber	fegato	hígado	fígado
Kaldaunen, Kutteln	trippa	callos	tripas
Muskel-/Kaumagen	ventriglio	molleja	moela
Zunge	lingua	lengua	língua
Flügelspitze	punta d'ala	punta del ala	asas
Hühnerhaut	pelle del pollo	piel de pollo	pele de frango
Fleischklößchen	polpette di carne	albóndigas de carne	almôndegas
Wachtelei	uovo di quaglia	huevo de codorniz	ovos de codorniz
Hühnerteile mit **Wasabi**	pezzi di pollo con **wasabi**	trozos de pollo con **wasabi**	porções de frango com **wasabi**

SOBA -YA MENU

蕎麦

JAPANESE	ENGLISH	FRANÇAIS
hiya-mugi	medium wheat noodles dipped in cold broth	nouilles moyennes de froment servies froides
kake-soba / -udon	noodles in plain, hot broth	nouilles dans bouillon chaud
kama-age-udon	**udon** dipped in hot broth	**udon** trempé dans bouillon chaud
kamo-namban -soba / -udon	noodles + duck + leek (lit. barbarian-style duck)	nouilles + canard + poireau (lit. canard à la barbare)
karē-udon	**udon** + curry sauce	**udon** à la sauce au curry
kitsune-soba / -udon	noodles + deep-fried **tōfu** (lit. fox's noodles)	nouilles + **tōfu** frit (lit. nouilles du renard)
mori-soba	**soba** dipped in cold broth	**soba** trempé dans bouillon froid
okame-soba / -udon	noodles + **kamaboko** + veg (in shape of face)	nouilles + **kamaboko** + légumes (en forme de visage)
sōmen	thin wheat noodles dipped in cold broth	fines nouilles de froment trempées dans bouillon froid
tanuki-soba / -udon	noodles + **tempura** batter (lit. badger's noodles)	nouilles + friture de **tempura** (lit. nouilles du blaireau)
tempura-soba / -udon	noodles + prawn **tempura**	nouilles + **tempura** de crevettes
tsukimi-soba / -udon	noodles + raw egg (lit. full moon noodles)	nouilles + œuf cru (lit. nouilles de pleine lune)
zaru-soba	**nori** + **soba** dipped in cold broth	**nori** + **soba** trempées dans bouillon froid

DEUTSCH	ITALIANO	ESPAÑOL	PORTUGUÊS
mitteldicke Weizennudeln in kalte Brühe getunkt	spaghetti medi di grano inzuppati in brodo freddo	fideos de trigo medianos mojados en caldo frío	massa média de trigo, molhada em caldo frio
Nudeln in klarer, heißer Brühe	spaghetti in brodo caldo	fideos en caldo caliente	caldo quente com massa
Udon in heiße Brühe getunkt	**udon** inzuppati in brodo caldo	**udon** mojados en caldo caliente	**udon** molhado em caldo quente
Nudeln + Ente + Lauch (wörtl. Ente nach Barbarenart)	spaghetti + anatra + porri (lett. anatra alla barbara)	fideos + pato + puerros (lit. pato a la bárbara)	massa + pato + alho porro (lit. pato à moda bárbara)
Udon + Currysoße	**udon** + salsa al curry	**udon** + salsa curry	**udon** + molho de caril
Nudeln + frittierter **Tōfu** (wörtl. Fuchsnudeln)	spaghetti + **tōfu** fritto (lett. spaghetti della volpe)	fideos + **tōfu** frito (lit. fideos del zorro)	massa + **tōfu** frito (lit. massa de raposa)
Soba in kalte Brühe getunkt	**soba** inzuppata in brodo freddo	**soba** mojada en caldo frío	**soba** molhada em caldo frio
Nudeln + **Kamaboko** + Gemüse (in Form eines Gesichts)	spaghetti + **kamaboko** + verdura (a forma di faccia)	fideos + **kamaboko** + verdura (con forma de rostro)	massa + **kamaboko** + legumes (em forma de rosto)
dünne Weizennudeln in kalte Brühe getunkt	spaghettini di grano inzuppati in brodo freddo	fideos delgados de trigo mojados en caldo frío	massa fina de trigo molhada em caldo frio
Nudeln + **Tempura**-Teig (wörtl. Dachsnudeln)	spaghetti + pastella **tempura** (lett. spaghetti del procione)	fideos + batido de **tempura** (lit. fideos del tejo)	massa + massa de filetes frita (lit. massa de texugo)
Nudeln + Garnelen-**Tempura**	spaghetti + **tempura** di gamperetti	fideos + **tempura** de langostino	massa + **tempura** de gambas
Nudeln + rohes Ei (wörtl. Vollmondnudeln)	spaghetti + uovo crudo (lett. spaghetti luna piena)	fideos + huevo crudo (lit. fideos de luna llena)	massa + ovo cru (lit. massa de lua cheia)
Nori + **Soba**, in kalte Brühe getunkt	**nori** + **soba** inzuppate in brodo freddo	**nori** + **soba** mojados en caldo frío	**nori** + **soba** molhados em caldo frio

CHŪKA MENU

中華

JAPANESE	ENGLISH	FRANÇAIS
chāhan	mixed fried rice	friture de riz mixte
chāshū-men	**rāmen** in broth + roast pork	**rāmen** servi dans bouillon + porc rôti
chūka-don	**domburi** of pork / prawn + veg	**domburi** de porc / crevettes + légumes
gyōza	fried crescent dumplings of meat + veg	beignets à la viande et aux légumes en forme de croissant
hiyashi-chūka	cold sweet & sour **rāmen** + ham + veg	**rāmen** aigre-doux froid + jambon + légumes
kata-yaki-soba	deep-fried egg noodles + meat + veg	nouilles aux œufs frites + viande + légumes
miso-rāmen	**rāmen** in **miso** broth	**rāmen** dans bouillon de **miso**
shio-rāmen	**rāmen** in salty broth	**rāmen** dans bouillon salé
subuta	sweet & sour pork	porc aigre-doux
tan-men	**shio-rāmen** + fried veg	**shio-rāmen** + légumes frits
tenshin-don	crab omelette **domburi**	**domburi** à l'omelette au crabe
ton-kotsu rāmen	**rāmen** in pork broth	**rāmen** dans bouillon au porc
yaki-soba	stir-fried egg noodles + meat + veg	nouilles aux œufs sautées avec viande + légumes

DEUTSCH	ITALIANO	ESPAÑOL	PORTUGUÊS
gebratener gemischter Reis	riso misto fritto	arroz frito mixto	misto frito arroz
Rāmen in Brühe + Schweinebraten	**rāmen** in brodo + maiale arrosto	caldo con **rāmen** + carne de cerdo al horno	caldo de **rāmen** + porco assado
Domburi aus Schweinefl. / Garnele + Gemüse	**domburi** di maiale / gamberetti + verdura	**domburi** de carne de cerdo / langostino + verduras	**domburi** de porco / gambas + legumes
gebratene Hörnchen aus Fleisch + Gemüse	polpette fritte a mezzaluna di carne e verdura	bolas fritas con forma de media luna, rellenas de carne + verduras	empadas de carne + legumes fritas em forma de meia lua
kalte, süßsaure **Rāmen** + Schinken + Gemüse	**rāmen** agrodolce freddo + prosciutto + verdura	**rāmen** agridulce frío + jamón + verduras	**rāmen** frio agridoce + fiambre + legumes
frittierte Eiernudeln + Fleisch + Gemüse	spaghettini all'uovo fritti + carne + verdura	fideos de huevo fritos + carne + verduras	massa de ovos frita + carne + legumes
Rāmen in **Miso**suppe	**rāmen** in brodo di **miso**	caldo de **miso** con **rāmen**	caldo de **miso** com **rāmen**
Rāmen in salziger Brühe	**rāmen** in brodo salato	caldo salado con **rāmen**	caldo salgado com **rāmen**
süßsaures Schweinefleisch	maiale agrodolce	carne de cerdo agridulce	porco agridoce
Shio-Rāmen + gebratene Gemüse	**shio-rāmen** + verdura fritta	**shio-rāmen** + verduras fritas	**shio-rāmen** + legumes fritos
Krebsomelett **Domburi**	omelette **domburi** di granchio	**domburi** con tortilla de cangrejo	**domburi** omelete de caranguejo
Rāmen in Schweinefleischbrühe	**rāmen** in brodo di maiale	caldo de carne de cerde con **rāmen**	caldo de porco com **rāmen**
Eiernudeln + Fleisch + Gemüse unter Rühren gebraten	spaghettini all'uovo saltati + carne + verdura	sofrito de fideos de huevo + carne + verduras	massa de ovo frita + carne + legumes

おでん

JAPANESE	ENGLISH	FRANÇAIS
atsu-age	thick-sliced **tōfu**, deep-fried outside only	tranches épaisses de **tōfu**, saisies dans friture
chikuwa	steamed tube of fish + egg paste	tube de pâte cuite de poisson et d'œuf
daikon	white radish	radis japonais
gan-modoki	ball of deep-fried **tōfu** + veg (lit. mock wild goose)	**tōfu** + légumes frits (lit. fausse oie sauvage)
hampen	boiled cake of white fish + yam	boulette de poisson blanc + igname
ika-ten	deep-fried ball of squid + fish paste	croquette d'encornet frite + concentré de poisson
jaga-imo	potato	pomme de terre
kombu	kelp	varech
konnyaku	vegetarian jelly from devil's tongue plant	gelée végétarienne à base de plante
ninjin	carrot	carotte
tako	octopus	poulpe
tōfu	soybean curd	pâte de soja
yude tamago	boiled egg	œuf dur

ODEN MENU

DEUTSCH	ITALIANO	ESPAÑOL	PORTUGUÊS
dicke **Tōfu**scheiben, frittiert	**tōfu** tagliato spesso fritto solo esternamente	rodajas gruesas de **tōfu**, fritas muy ligeramente	fatias grossas de **tōfu**, ligeiramente fritas
gedämpfte Fisch- u. Eipastete	tubo vuoto di patè di uovo + pesce	manga de pasta de pescado y huevo, cocida al vapor	rolinho de pasta de ovo + peixe cozido a vapor
weißer Rettich	ravanello bianco	rábano blanco	rabanete branco
frittierter **Tōfu** + Gemüse (wörtl. falsche Wildgans)	palle fritte di **tōfu** + verdura (lett. oca selvatica finta)	**tōfu** frito + verduras (lit. ganso silvestre falso)	**tōfu** + legumes fritos
gekochter Kuchen aus weißem Fisch + Jamswurzel	polpetta di pesce + yam bollita	budín hervido de pescado blanco + ñame	bolo de peixe branco + inhame cozido
frittierte Bällchen aus Kalmar + Fischpastete	polpetta fritta di patè di pesce + calamaro	albóndiga frita de pasta de calamar + pescado	bola de lulas + pasta de peixe frita
Kartoffel	patata	patata	batata
Kelpalge	alga marina	algas marinas	algas
vegetarisches Gelee aus Konnyaku	gelatina vegetariana dalla pianta lingua di diavolo	gelatina vegetariana (extraída de la planta lengua del diablo)	gelatina vegetariana feita com uma espécie de inhame
Karotte	carota	zanahoria	cenoura
Oktopus, Polyp	polipo	pulpo	polvo
Tofu, Sojabohnenquark	semi di soia raccagliati	cuajada de semilla de soja	soja coalhada
gekochtes Ei	uovo bollito	huevo duro	ovo cozido

JAPANESE	ENGLISH	FRANÇAIS
bīru	beer	bière
chūhai	**shōchū** + soda water + flavouring syrup	**shōchū** + eau de Seltz + sirop aromatisé
kō-cha	English-style tea	thé anglais
kōhī	coffee	café
mat-cha	foamy green tea for tea ceremony	thé vert mousseux pour cérémonie du thé
mizu	water	eau
mizuwari	whisky + water	whisky + eau
nihon-shu	**sake**, brewed rice wine	**sake**, alcool de riz
o-cha	tea, usually green	thé, généralement vert
orenji-jūsu	orange squash / juice	orangeade / jus d'orange
shōchū	strong spirit made from grain / potato	alcool fort de grain / pomme de terre
ume-shu	sweet liqueur of **shōchū** + Japanese apricot	liqueur de **shōchū** + abricot japonais
ūron-cha	Chinese oolong tea	thé chinois oolong

飲物

DEUTSCH	ITALIANO	ESPAÑOL	PORTUGUÊS
Bier	birra	cerveza	cerveja
Shōchū + Sodawasser + Sirup	**shōchū** + acqua di seltz + sciroppo aromatico	**shōchū** + soda + jarabe aromatizante	**shōchū** + água gaseificada + xarope aromatizante
engl. Tee	tè di Ceylon al latte	té inglés	chá servido à maneira inglesa
Kaffee	caffè	café	café
schäumender grüner Tee f. Teezeremonie	tè verde schiumoso per la cerimonia del tè	té verde espumoso para la ceremonia del té	chá para a cerimónia de chá
Wasser	acqua	agua	água
Whisky + Wasser	whisky annacquato	whisky + agua	whisky + água
Sake, gebrauter Reiswein	**sake**, vino di riso fermentato	**sake**, vino fuerte de arroz	**sake**, aguardente de arroz
Tee, meist grün	tè, di solito verde	té, generalmente verde	chá, normalmente verde
Orangenlimonade /–saft	aranciata / succo di arancio	zumo de naranja / naranjada	sumo de laranja (natural / diluído)
Korn-/ Kartoffelschnaps	alcol forte fatto da grano / patate	aguardiente a base de cereal / patata	bebida alcoólica forte feita de cereais / batata
süßer Likör aus **Shōchū** + jap. Aprikose	liquore dolce di **shōchū** + albicocca giapponese	licor dulce de **shōchū** + albaricoque japonés	licor doce de **shōchū** + alperce japonês
Chinescher Oolong-Tee	tè cinese di tipo oolong	té chino oolong	chá oolong chinês

En Glossary
F Glossaire
D Glossar
I Glossario
Es Glosario
P Glossário

JAPANESE	ENGLISH	FRANÇAIS
abura-age	thin-sliced **tōfu**, deep-fried	tranches fines de **tōfu** frites
ae-mono, -ae	fish / veg + thick dressing	poisson / légumes + sauce épaisse
age-dashi-dōfu	**shōyu** + ginger + deep-fried, floured **tōfu**	**tōfu** pané et frit + **shōyu** + gingembre
age-mono, -age	deep-fried	frit
ankō-nabe	**nabe-mono** of simmered monkfish	**nabe-mono** mijoté avec lotte
asari-jiru	clam + **miso** soup	soupe de palourde + **miso**
atsu-age	thick-sliced **tōfu**, deep-fried outside only	grosses tranches de **tōfu** saisies dans friture
beni-shōga	red pickled ginger	gingembre dans marinade rouge
bentō	boxed meal, originally for take-away	repas en boîte, parfois à emporter
buri	yellowtail (fish)	sériole
buta-niku	pork	porc
buta no kaku-ni	braised pork belly	poitrine de porc braisée
chanko-nabe	mixed **nabe-mono** for sumo wrestlers	**nabe-mono** varié pour lutteurs de sumo

言葉

DEUTSCH	ITALIANO	ESPAÑOL	PORTUGUÊS
dünne, frittierte **Tōfu**scheiben	**tōfu** fritto tagliato fine	lonchas delgadas de **tōfu**, fritas	**tōfu** frito cortado em fatias finas
Fisch / Gemüse + dickflüssige Marinade	pesce / verdura + condimento denso	pescado / verduras + aliño espeso	peixe / legumes fritos + cobertura espessa
Shōyu + Ingwer + frittierter **Tōfu**	**tōfu** infarinato e fritto + **shōyu** + zenzero	**shōyu** + jengibre + **tōfu** enharinado y frito	**shōyu** + gengibre + **tōfu** frito passado por farinha
frittiert	fritto	frito en aceite abundante	frito
Nabe-mono aus gekochtem Seeteufel	**nabe-mono** di coda di rospo sobbollito	**nabe-mono** de rape cocido a fuego lento	**nabe-mono** de tamboril fervido
Suppe aus Sandklaffmuschel + **Miso**	minestra di **miso** + vongole	sopa de almejas + **miso**	sopa **miso** + amêijoa
dicke, **Tōfu**scheiben, frittiert	**tōfu** tagliato spesso fritto solo esternamente	rodajas gruesas de **tōfu**, fritas muy ligeramente	**tōfu** frito ligeiramente, cortado em fatias grossas
rot eingelegter Ingwer	zenzero in aceto rosso	jengibre en escabeche rosado	gengibre em pickle
Mahlzeit im Kästchen, urspr. z. Mitnehmen	pasto in scatola, in origine era da portare via	comida en una caja, originalmente para llevar	refeição embalada; originalmente para take-away
Gelbschwanz (Fisch)	ricciola, leccia	sorel, lenguado	linguado
Schweinefleisch	maiale	carne de cerdo	porco
geschmorter Schweinebauch	stufato di pancetta	panceta de cerdo braseada	barriga de porco estufada
gemischtes **Nabe-mono** für Sumo-Ringer	**nabe-mono** misto per lottatori sumo	**nabe-mono** mixto para luchadores de sumo	**nabe-mono** misto para lutadores de *sumo*

JAPANESE	ENGLISH	FRANÇAIS
cha-soba	**soba** made of green tea	**soba** au thé vert
chawan-mushi	steamed egg custard + chicken / prawn / gingko nut	crème d'œufs + poulet / crevettes / noix de gingko
chō-shoku	breakfast	petit-déjeuner
chūka	Japanized Chinese food	cuisine chinoise accommodée à la japonaise
chū-shoku	lunch	déjeuner
daikon-oroshi	grated white radish	radis japonais râpé
dashi	stock, usually kelp / **katsuo-bushi**	bouillon, généralement de varech / **katsuo-bushi**
dengaku	grilled, skewered fish / **tōfu** / veg + **miso**	brochette de poisson grillé / **tōfu** / légumes + **miso**
dezāto	dessert	dessert
dobin-mushi	clear soup + chicken / fish / veg, in teapot	consommé au poulet / poisson / légumes, servi dans théière
domburi, -don	bowl of rice + meat / veg / fish topping	bol de riz + garniture de viande / légumes / poisson
ebi	prawn	crevette
fugu	puffer fish, blowfish	poisson-globe

DEUTSCH	ITALIANO	ESPAÑOL	PORTUGUÊS
Soba mit Grüntee im Nudelteig	**soba** di tè verde	**soba** de té verde	**soba** de chá verde
gedämpfte Eierspeise + Huhn / Garnelen / Gingkonuß	crema all'uovo a vapore + pollo / gamberetto / noce ginkgo	cuajadas de huevo + pollo / langostino / nuez de gingko	creme de ovo em vapor + frango / gamba / noz de gincgo
Frühstück	colazione	desayuno	pequeno-almoço
japanisierte chinesische Speisen	cibo cinese fatto alla giapponese	comida china adaptada al gusto japonés	comida chinêsa de estilo japonês
Mittagessen	pranzo	almuerzo	almoço
geriebener weißer Rettich	ravanello bianco grattugiato	rábano blanco rallado	rabanete branco ralado
Brühe, meist Kelpalge / **Katsuo-bushi**	brodo, di solito di alghe / **katsuo-bushi**	caldo, generalmente de alga marina / **katsuo-bushi**	caldo, normalmente algas / **katsuo-bushi**
Fisch / **Tōfu** / Gemüse am Spieß gegrillt + **Miso**	spiedino di pesce / **tōfu** / verdura alla griglia + **miso**	brochetas de pescado / **tōfu** / verduras + **miso**	grelhadas de peixe / **tōfu** / legumes + **miso**
Nachspeise	dessert	postre	sobremesa
klare Suppe + Huhn / Fisch / Gemüse, in der Teekanne	consommé + pollo / pesce / vedura in una teiera	caldo ligero + pollo / pescado / verduras, en tetera	sopa clara + frango / peixe / legumes, em bule
eine Schüssel Reis + Fleisch / Gemüse / Fisch	ciotola di riso cosparso con carne / verdura / pesce	bol de arroz cubierto de carne / verdura / pescado	taça de arroz + cobertura de carne / legumes / peixe
Königsgarnele, Riesengarnele	gamberetto	langostino	gamba
Kugelfisch	pesce palla	pez globo, tamboril	peixe baiaco

JAPANESE	ENGLISH	FRANÇAIS
furai	deep-fried, breaded	pané et frit
gohan	boiled rice	riz nature
goma	sesame	sésame
gyū-don	beef **domburi**	**domburi** au bœuf
gyū-niku	beef	bœuf
hakusai	Chinese cabbage	choux chinois
harusame	bean / potato flour vermicelli (lit. spring rain)	vermicelles de farine de haricot / pomme de terre
hashi	chopsticks	baguettes
higawari teishoku	set meals of the day	menu fixe changé quotidiennement
hiya-yakko	cold **tōfu** + ginger + **katsuo-bushi**	**tōfu** froid + gingembre + **katsuo-bushi**
ichimi tōgarashi	red chilli powder	poudre de piment rouge
ika	squid	encornet, seiche
ikura-oroshi	salmon roe + grated radish	œufs de saumon + radis râpé

DEUTSCH	ITALIANO	ESPAÑOL	PORTUGUÊS
paniert, frittiert	impanato e fritto	rebozado y frito en aceite abundante	panado
gekochter Reis	riso bollito	arroz hervido	arroz cozido
Sesam	sesamo	sésamo	sésamo
Rindfleisch **Domburi**	**domburi** di manzo	**domburi** de ternera	**domburi** de carne de vaca
Rindfleisch	manzo	carne de ternera	carne de vaca
Chinakohl	cavolo cinese	col china	couve chinesa
Fadennudeln aus Bohnen-/Kartoffelmehl (wörtl. Frühlingsregen)	vermicelli di farina di fagioli / patate (lett. pioggia primaverile)	fideos de harina de habas / patata (lit. lluvia de primavera)	aletria de farinha de batata / feijão (lit. chuva de Primavera)
Eßstäbchen	bastoncini	palillos	pauzinhos
Tagesmenü	variante del giorno del menù fisso	menú fijo que varía cada día	pratos do dia
kalter **Tōfu** + Ingwer + **Katsuo-bushi**	**tōfu** freddo + zenzero + **katsuo-bushi**	**tōfu** frío + jengibre + **katsuo-bushi**	**tōfu** frio + gengibre + **katsuo-bushi**
rotes Chilipulver	peperoncino rosso in polvere	guindilla (ají picante) en polvo	pó de pimentón vermelho
Kalmar	calamaro, totano	calamar, sepia	lula
Lachsrogen + geriebener Rettich	uova di salmone + ravanello grattugiato	huevas de salmón + rábano rallado	ovas de salmão + rabanete ralado

JAPANESE	ENGLISH	FRANÇAIS
ippin ryōri	à la carte (lit. single dish cuisine)	à la carte (lit. cuisine à plat unique)
izaka-ya	pub with cheap food & drink	bar servant de la nourriture et des boissons bon marché
jaga-imo, imo	potato	pomme de terre
kaba-yaki	charcoal-grilled fish, usually eel	poisson grillé sur charbon de bois, généralement anguille
kai, -gai	shellfish, molluscs	coquillages
kaiseki ryōri	tea ceremony meal / formal haute cuisine	repas de cérémonie du thé / haute cuisine formelle
kaki	oyster	huître
kamaboko	steamed fishpaste loaf	pain de purée de poisson cuit à la vapeur
kanten	agar-agar vegetarian jelly	gelée végétarienne d'agar-agar
kappō	informal high class restaurant	restaurant de grand standing mais informel
kara-age	deep-fried, floured	fariné et frit
karashi	hot mustard	moutarde forte
karē-raisu	rice + curry sauce of meat / fish / veg	riz + sauce au curry avec viande / poisson / légumes

DEUTSCH	ITALIANO	ESPAÑOL	PORTUGUÊS
à la carte (wörtl. Einzelgerichte)	alla carta (lett. cucina dei piatti unici)	a la carta (lit. cocina de plato único)	à escolha (lit. cozinha de pratos individuais)
Gaststätte f. preisgünstiges Essen u. Getränke	pub con cibo e bevande a buon prezzo	bar-restaurante donde sirven bebidas y comida económicas	bar com comida e bebida económicas
Kartoffel	patata	patata	batata
Fisch, meist Aal, vom Holzkohlengrill	pesce alla brace, di solito anguilla	pescado asado a la barbacoa, normalmente anguila	peixe na brasa, normalmente enguia
Schalentier	mollusco	molusco	marisco de concha
Teezeremonie / formelle feine Küche	pasto con cerimonia del tè / alta cucina formale	cocina de categoría / comida que acompaña la ceremonia del té	refeição com cerimónia de chá / alta cozinha formal
Auster	ostrica	ostra	ostra
gedämpfte Fischpastete	panetto di patè di pesce cotto a vapore	budín de pasta de pescado, cocido al vapor	pão de pasta de peixe cozido a vapor
Agar-Agar	gelatina vegetariana agar-agar	gelatina vegetariana hecha con agar-agar	gelatina vegetariana agar-agar
gemütliches, feines Restaurant	ristorante di alta classe informale	restaurante de categoría pero de carácter informal	restaurante informal de classe elevada
in Mehl gewendet + frittiert	infarinato e fritto	enharinado y frito en aceite abundante	frito, passado por farinha
scharfer Senf	mostarda / senape calda	mostaza picante	mostarda picante
Reis + Fleisch / Fisch / Gemüse-Curry	riso + salsa di carne / pesce / verdura al curry	arroz + salsa curry con carne / pescado / verduras	arroz + caril de carne / peixe / legumes

JAPANESE	ENGLISH	FRANÇAIS
katsu	deep-fried, breaded meat / fish	viande / poisson pané(e) et frit(e)
katsu-don	**ton-katsu** + egg **domburi**	**domburi** au **ton-katsu** + œuf
katsuo-bushi	dried bonito (fish), for flavouring	bonite sèche, utilisée comme condiment
katsuo no tataki	seared raw bonito + ginger + vinegar / **shōyu**	bonite saisie + gingembre + vinaigre / **shōyu**
kayaku-gohan	chopped meat / fish / veg, boiled with rice	émincé de viande / poisson / légumes, cuit avec du riz
kimpira gobō	sweet, stir-fried burdock + **shōyu** + sesame	bardane sautée dans sauce sucrée + **shōyu** + sésame
kishimen	flat **udon** from Nagoya region	**udon** plates, région de Nagoya
konnyaku	vegetarian jelly from devil's tongue plant	gelée végétarienne à base de plante
koshō	ground white pepper	poivre blanc moulu
kuri	sweet chestnuts	châtaignes
kushi-age	deep-fried, breaded skewers of meat / fish / veg	brochettes de viande poisson / légumes / poisson panées et frites
kyūri	cucumber	concombre
maki-zushi, -maki	roll of **sushi** + **nori**	**sushi** en forme de rouleau avec **nori**

DEUTSCH	ITALIANO	ESPAÑOL	PORTUGUÊS
Fleisch / Fisch paniert + frittiert	carne / pesce impanato e fritto	carne / pescado rebozados y fritos	carne / peixe panados
Ton-katsu + Ei **Domburi**	**domburi** di **ton-katsu** all'uovo	**domburi** de **ton-katsu** + huevo	**domburi** de **ton-katsu** + ovo
getrockneter Bonito (Fisch), als Würzmittel	tonno bonita seccato, per insaporire	bonito desecado, usado como condimento	voador secas, para dar sabor
roher Bonito + Ingwer + Essig / **Shōyu**	bonita rosolato + zenzero + aceto / **shōyu**	bonito crudo + jengibre + vinagre / **shōyu**	voador cruas + gengibre + vinagre / **shōyu**
Fleisch / Fisch / Gemüse, gehackt u.m. Reis gekocht	carne / pesce / verdura battuti, bolliti con riso	carne / pescado / verduras picados, hervidos con arroz	peixe / carne / legumes aos bocados, cozidos c/ arroz
süße gebratene Klette + **Shōyu** + Sesam	bardana dolce saltata + **shōyu** + sesamo	sofrito dulce de bardana + **shōyu** + sésamo	bardana salteada + **shōyu** + sésamo
Bandnudel **Udon** aus Nagoya	**udon** sottile della regione Nagoya	**udon** planos, típicos de la región de Nagoya	**udon** liso, região de Nagoya
Konnyaku	gelatina vegetariana dalla pianta lingua di diavolo	lengua de diablo (planta)	gelatina vegetariana, espécie de inhame
gemahlener weißer Pfeffer	pepe bianco in polvere	pimienta blanca molida	pimenta branca moída
Eßkastanien	castagne dolci	castañas dulces	castanha doce
Fleisch / Fisch / Gemüse am Spieß, paniert + frittiert	spiedini impanati e fritti di carne / pesce / verdura	brochetas rebozadas y fritas de / carne / pescado verduras	espetadas panadas de carne / peixe / legumes
Gurke	cetriolo	pepino	pepino
Rolle aus **Sushi** + **Nori**	**sushi** + **nori** arrotolati	rollo de **sushi** + **nori**	rolinho de **sushi** + **nori**

JAPANESE	ENGLISH	FRANÇAIS
makunouchi bentō	**bentō** of rice + ten kinds of food	**bentō** de riz + dix types d'ingrédients
matsuzaka gyū	marbled beef	bœuf marbré
maze-gohan	meat / fish / veg mixed with boiled rice	mélange de viande / poisson / légumes et riz nature
men, -men	any noodles	nouilles
mirin	sweet alcoholic flavouring	arôme sucré alcoolisé
miso	fermented paste of soybean + grain	pâte de graines de soja fermentées
miso-shiru	**miso** soup	soupe au **miso**
mochi	glutinous rice cake	boulette de riz glutineux
momiji-oroshi	grated white radish + red chilli	radis japonais + piment rouge râpés
mori-awase	assortment	assortiment
mozuku	thread-like seaweed	algues très fines
mushi-mono, -mushi	steamed	cuit à la vapeur
nabe-mono, -nabe	dish cooked in one pot, often at table	plat cuit dans un pot, souvent devant les convives

DEUTSCH	ITALIANO	ESPAÑOL	PORTUGUÊS
Bentō aus Reis + zehn Speisen	**bentō** di riso + dieci tipi di cibo	**bentō** de arroz + diez tipos de comida	**bentō** de arroz + dez tipos de comida
durchzogenes Rindfleisch	manzo nel mezzo grasso	carne de vaca veteada	carne de vaca marmoreada
Fleisch / Fisch / Gemüse m. Reis vermischt	carne / pesce / verdura mischiati a riso bollito	carne / pescado / verduras mezclados con arroz hervido	carne / peixe / legumes misturados c/ arroz cozido
Nudeln	spaghetti	fideos o tallarines	massa
süßes alkoholisches Würzmittel	aromi alcolici dolci	aromatizante alcohólico dulce	aromatizante doce alcoólico
fermentierte Paste aus Soja + Getreide	pasta fermentata di seme di soia + grano	pasta de germen de soja + grano fermentada	puré de soja + cereal fermentado
Misosuppe	minestra di **miso**	sopa de **miso**	sopa **miso**
Klebereisklößchen	polpetta di riso glutinosa	pastelillo de arroz glutinoso	bolo de arroz glutinoso
geriebener weißer Rettich + roter Chili	ravanello bianco + peperoncino rosso grattati	rábano blanco + guindilla rallados	rabanete branco + pimentão vermelho ralados
Auswahl, Mischung	assortimento	selección	sortido
Mozuku, fadenartige Alge	alghe marine filamentose	algas marinas con aspecto de hilo	alga semelhante a um fio
gedämpft	cotto a vapore	cocido al vapor	em vapor
Eintopfgericht, oft am Tisch gekocht	piatto cotto in una pentola, spesso al tavolo	cocido, a menudo preparado en la mesa	prato cozinhado num tacho, muitas vezes à mesa

JAPANESE	ENGLISH	FRANÇAIS
nattō	fermented soy beans	graines de soja fermentées
nattsu	nuts	noix, noisettes, etc
negi	spring onions, welsh onions	ciboule
niku	meat	viande
niku-jaga	simmered meat + potato	viande + pommes de terre mijotées
ni-mono, -ni	simmered / braised	mijoté / braisé
nin-niku	garlic	ail
nomi-mono	drinks	boissons
nomi-ya	bar	bar
nori	dried laver seaweed	algue marine séchée
o-	polite prefix	préfixe de politesse
o-cha-zuke	rice + tea / broth + shredded fish / pickles	riz + thé / bouillon + émincé de poissons / pickles
oden	stewed **nabe-mono** of **tōfu** + veg + fishcake	**nabe-mono** mijoté avec **tōfu** + légumes + croquette de poisson

DEUTSCH	ITALIANO	ESPAÑOL	PORTUGUÊS
fermentierte Sojabohnen	semi di soia fermentati	semillas de soja fermentadas	soja fermentada
Nüsse	noci	nueces	nozes, amendoins, etc
Frühlingszwiebeln	cipolline	cebolletas	cebolinho
Fleisch	carne	carne	carne
gekochtes Fleisch + Kartoffel	carne + patata sobbollite	carne + patatas cocidos a fuego lento	carne + batata fervida
gekocht, gegart	sobbollito / stufato	cocido a fuego lento / estofado	fervido / estufado
Knoblauch	aglio	ajo	alho
Getränke	bevande	bebidas	bebidas
Bar	bar	bar	bar
Nori, getrocknete Laver-Alge	alga della porpora, seccata	alga marina seca	alga seca
höfliche Vorsilbe	prefisso, indica cortesia	prefijo de cortesía	prefixo de cortesia
Reis + Tee / Brühe + zerpflückter Fisch / Pickles	riso + tè / brodo + julienne di pesce / sottaceti	arroz + té / caldo + pescado / encurtidos picados	arroz + chá / caldo + pickles / peixe em tirinhas
Nabe-mono aus Tōfu + Gemüse + Fischlaibchen	stufato nabe-mono di tōfu + verdura + polpette di pesce	nabe-mono de tōfu + verdura + bola de pescado	nabe-mono estufado de tōfu + legumes + bolo de peixe

JAPANESE	ENGLISH	FRANÇAIS
o-fu, -bu	wheat gluten	gluten de blé
ohitashi	cold roll of spinach + dressing	rouleau froid d'épinard avec assaisonnement
o-kashi,-gashi	confectionery / cakes / rice crackers	sucreries / pâtisseries / gâteaux de riz
o-kayu, -gayu	rice gruel	gruau de riz
okazu	any dish to accompany rice	tout plat servi avec du riz
okonomi-yaki	thick savoury pancake, cooked at table	crêpe épaisse salée, cuite devant les convives
o-makase	chef's choice meal	sélection du chef
o-nigiri, o-musubi	hand-held balls of rice + fish / veg filling	boulettes de riz farcies de poisson / légumes
o-suimono	clear soup	consommé
o-susume	recommendation	recommandation
o-tōshi, tsukidashi	hors d'œuvre, often complimentary	hors-d'œuvre, souvent gratuits
oyako-don	chicken + egg **domburi** (lit. parent + child)	**domburi** au poulet + œuf (lit. parent et enfant)
o-zendate	place setting	à table

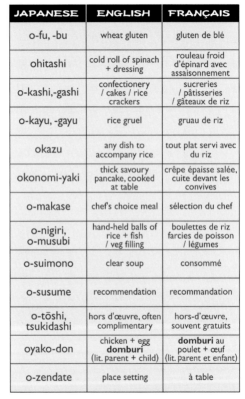

DEUTSCH	ITALIANO	ESPAÑOL	PORTUGUÊS
Weizengluten	glutine di grano	gluten de trigo	glúten de trigo
kalte Rolle aus Spinat + Marinade	involtino freddo di spinaci + condimento	rollo frío de espinacas + aliño	rolinho frio de espinafre + guarnição
Konfekt / Kuchen / Reiscracker	dolci / paste / cracker di riso	confites / pasteles / galletas de arroz	doçaria / bolos / bolachas de arroz
dünner Reisbrei	farinata di riso	gachas de arroz	papa de arroz
jede Speise, zu der Reis paßt	qualsiasi piatto di contorno al riso	cualquier plato para acompañar el arroz	qualquer prato que acompanhe arroz
dicker, salziger Pfannkuchen, am Tisch zubereitet	frittella spessa salata cotta al tavolo	crêpe o torta salada gruesa, frita en la mesa	panqueca salgada e espessa, cozinhada à mesa
Empfehlung des Kochs	pasto scelto dallo chef	menu escogido por el chef	selecção do chefe
Reisbällchen m. Fisch / Gemüse gefüllt, mit der Hand zu essen	palle di riso + pesce / verdura da mangiare in mano	bolas de arroz + relleno de pescado / verduras	bolinhas de arroz + recheio de legumes / peixe
klare Suppe	brodo, consommé	caldo, sopa clara	sopa clara
Empfehlung	consiglio	recomendación	recomendação
Vorspeise, oft gratis	stuzzichini, spesso gratis	entremeses, a menudo obsequio de la casa	canapés, muitas vezes complemento
Huhn + Ei **Domburi** (wörtl. Eltern + Kind)	**domburi** di gallina all'uovo (lett. chioccia e pulcino)	**domburi** de pollo + huevo (lit. madre e hijo)	**domburi** de galinha + ovo (lit. mãe e filho)
Gedeck	apparecchiato	lugar de la comida	mesa da refeição

JAPANESE	ENGLISH	FRANÇAIS
ponzu	citrus juice, used in sauce	sauce au jus de citron
rāmen	wheat + egg noodles, served with broth	nouilles de froment et aux œufs, servies avec bouillon
ranchi	lunch	déjeuner
robata-yaki	style of grilling in front of diners (lit. hearthside)	grillades préparées devant les convives (lit. foyer)
ryōri	cuisine, cookery	cuisine
ryō-tei	traditional haute cuisine restaurant	restaurant servant de la haute cuisine traditionnelle
saba	mackerel	maquereau
sakana, -zakana	fish	poisson
sake, -zake	brewed rice wine	alcool de riz fermenté
sanma	saury, mackerel pike	orphie maquereau
sansai	seasonal plants (lit. mountain vegetables)	plantes saisonnières (lit. légumes de montagne)
sanshō	bitter peppery spice	épice poivrée et amère
sashimi	raw fish / meat	poisson / viande cru(e)

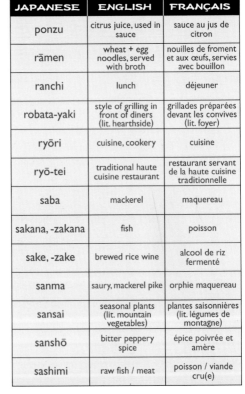

DEUTSCH	ITALIANO	ESPAÑOL	PORTUGUÊS
Zitronensaft, z. Tunken	succo di limone giapponese, per salse	zumo de cítrico, usado en salsas	sumo de citrino, para molho
Eiernudeln in Brühe	spaghettini all'uovo serviti con brodo	fideos de huevo + trigo servidos con caldo	massa de ovo + trigo, servidos com caldo
Mittagessen	pranzo	almuerzo	almoço
Grillzubereitung vor d. Gast (wörtl. am Kamin)	cottura alla griglia davanti ai clienti (lett. al camino)	asado frente a los comensales (lit. junto al fogón)	forma de grelhar a comida à frente dos convivas (lit. numa cozinha a carvão)
Küche, Kochkunst	cucina, arte culinaria	arte de cocinar	cozinha, culinária
traditionelles feines Restaurant	ristorante tradizionale di alta cucina	restaurante de alta cocina de tipo tradicional	restaurante de alta cozinha tradicional
Makrele	sgombro, macarello	caballa	cavala, cavalinha
Fisch	pesce	pescado	peixe
gebrauter Reiswein	vino di riso fermentato ad alta gradazione	vino fuerte de arroz	aguardente de arroz
Kurzschnabel-Makrelenhecht	gastaurello	paparda (pescado)	tira-vira
Pflanzen in Saison (wörtl. Berggemüse)	piante di stagione (lett. verdure montane)	plantas de temporada (lit. verduras de la montaña)	plantas da época (lit. legumes da montanha)
bitteres, pfeffriges Gewürz	spezia peposa amara	condimento amargo y picante	especiaria amarga apimentada
roher Fisch / rohes Fleisch	carne / pesce crudi	pescado / carne crudos	peixe / carne crus

JAPANESE	ENGLISH	FRANÇAIS
satō	sugar	sucre
satsuma-age	deep-fried fishcake	croquette de poisson frite
satsuma-imo	sweet potato	patate douce
setto	set meal	menu fixe
shabu-shabu	beef + veg dipped in boiling stock at table	bœuf et légumes plongés dans bouillon chaud
shichimi tōgarashi	seven spice chilli powder	poudre pimentée aux sept épices
shime-saba	mackerel soused in salt + vinegar	maquereau mariné dans du sel + vinaigre
shio	salt	sel
shio-yaki	grilled with salt	grillé avec couche de sel
shirataki	**konnyaku** noodles, without gluten (lit. white waterfalls)	nouilles **konnyaku** sans gluten (lit. cascades blanches)
shiru, -jiru	soup	soupe
shiso, me-jiso	beefsteak plant, like peppery mint	herbe aromatique, sorte de menthe poivrée
shōga	ginger	gingembre

DEUTSCH	ITALIANO	ESPAÑOL	PORTUGUÊS
Zucker	zucchero	azúcar	açúcar
frittiertes Fischlaibchen	polpette di pesce fritte	torta frita de pescado	bolo de peixe frito
Süßkartoffel	ipomea, patata dolce	boniato, batata dulce	batata doce
Menü	pasto fisso	plato combinado	ementa fixa
Rind + Gemüse Fondue in Brühe	manzo + verdure inzuppate in brodo bollente al tavolo	carne de ternera + verduras que se sumergen en caldo hirviente	carne de vaca + legumes mergulhados em caldo a ferver
Chilipulver mit sieben Gewürzen	polvere di peperoncino alle sette spezie	condimento a base de siete especias	pó de sete especiarias
in Salz + Essig eingelegte Makrele	macarello in salamoia di sale + aceto	caballa adobada con sal + vinagre	cavala em salmoura + vinagre
Salz	sale	sal	sal
gegrillt mit Salz	alla brace con sale	asado a la brasa con sal	grelhado com sal
Konnyaku Nudeln, glutenfrei (wörtl. weißer Wasserfall)	spaghettini **konnyaku** senza glutine (lett. cascate bianche)	fideos **konnyaku**, exentos de gluten (lit. cascadas blancas)	massa **konnyaku**, sem glúten (lit. cascatas brancas)
Suppe	minestra	sopa	sopa
Shiso Perilla	menta perilla, pepolino	hierba aromática parecida a la menta	erva aromática tipo hortelã
Ingwer	zenzero	jengibre	gengibre

JAPANESE	ENGLISH	FRANÇAIS
shōjin ryōri	vegan Buddhist cuisine (lit. path of purity)	cuisine végétalienne bouddhiste (lit. voie de la pureté)
shōkadō bentō	formal **bentō** of four kinds of food	**bentō** de cuisine formelle aux quatre plats
shōyu	soy sauce	sauce de soja
soba	wheat + buckwheat noodles, usually with broth	nouilles de froment et de sarrasin
sōsu	any brown sauce	toute sauce brune
suki-yaki	**nabe-mono** of beef + veg + **shirataki**	**nabe-mono** avec bœuf + légumes + **shirataki**
suno-mono, -su	fish / veg + vinegar dressing	poisson / légumes avec vinaigrette
sushi, -zushi	vinegared rice + fish / veg, often raw	riz au vinaigre avec poisson / légumes souvent servis crus
tai	red sea bream	daurade, vivandeau
takikomi-gohan	meat / fish / veg boiled with rice	viande / poisson / légumes cuits avec du riz
tako-yaki	griddled balls of batter + octopus	petits beignets de poulpe cuits sur plaque en fonte
tamago	egg	œuf
tamago-don	egg **domburi**	**domburi** à l'œuf

DEUTSCH	ITALIANO	ESPAÑOL	PORTUGUÊS
vegan. buddhist. Küche (wörtl. Pfad d. Reinheit)	cucina vegana Buddista (lett. sentiero di purezza)	cocina vegetariana budista (lit. camino de la pureza)	cozinha vegetariana budista (lit. caminho da pureza)
Formelles **Bentō** mit vier Speisen	**bentō** formale di quattro tipi di cibo	**bentō** formal, cuatro tipos de comida	**bentō** formal de quatro tipos de comida
Sojasoße	salsa di soia	salsa de soja	molho de soja
Weizen- + Buchweizennudeln, meist in Brühe	spaghettini di grano + grano saraceno di solito con brodo	fideos de trigo + alforfón, generalmente con caldo	massa de trigo mourisco, normalmente com caldo
jede braune Soße	salsa scura qualsiasi	cualquier salsa marrón	qualquer molho castanho
Nabe-mono aus Rind + Gemüse **+ Shirataki**	**nabe-mono** di carne + verdura **+ shirataki**	**nabe-mono** de ternera + verduras **+ shirataki**	**nabe-mono** de vaca + legumes **+ shirataki**
Fisch / Gemüse + Essigmarinade	pesce / verdura + condimento all'aceto	pescado / verduras + vinagreta	peixe / legumes + tempero de vinagre
marinierter Reis + Fisch / Gemüse, oft roh	riso all'aceto + pesce / verdura spesso crudi	arroz con vinagre + pescado / verduras, a menudo crudos	arroz avinagrado + peixe / legumes muitas vezes crus
Nordische Seebrasse	dentice, orata, triglia di scoglio	besugo	pargo, goraz
Fleisch / Fisch / Gemüse, m. d. Reis gekocht	carne / pesce / verdura bollita con riso	carne / pescado / verduras hervidos con arroz	carne / peixe / legumes cozidos c/ arroz
Oktopus im Backteig, auf heißer Eisenplatte gebraten	arancini grigliati di pastella + polipo	albóndigas de pulpo + batido, cocinadas en una plancha	bolinhas de polvo em massa de filete
Ei	uova	huevo	ovo
Ei **Domburi**	**domburi** all'uovo	**domburi** de huevo	**domburi** de ovo

JAPANESE	ENGLISH	FRANÇAIS
tama-negi	onion	oignon
tare, -dare	chef's sweet sauce, usually with **shōyu** / **mirin**	sauce légèrement sucrée, souvent avec **shōyu** / **mirin**
teishoku	set meal	menu fixe
temaki-zushi	cone-shaped **maki-zushi**	cornet de **maki-zushi**
tempura	deep-fried, battered prawns / fish / veg	beignets de crevettes / poisson / légumes
ten-don	**domburi** with **tempura**	**domburi** au **tempura**
ten-jū	lacquer box of **tempura** + rice	boîte lacquée contenant **tempura** + riz
ten-tsuyu	clear broth for dipping **tempura**	consommé pour tremper **tempura**
teppan-yaki	fried on hot iron plate set in table	frit sur plaque d'acier aménagée dans la table
teri-yaki	grilled & glazed with sweet sauce	grillé avec sauce légèrement sucrée
tōfu, -dōfu	soybean curd	pâte de soja
ton-jiru	**miso** soup with pork + veg	soupe de **miso** avec porc + légumes
ton-katsu	deep-fried, breaded pork cutlet	côtelette de porc panée et frite

DEUTSCH	ITALIANO	ESPAÑOL	PORTUGUÊS
Zwiebel	cipolla	cebolla	cebola
süße Soße des Kochs, meist mit **Shōyu / Mirin**	salsa dolce dello chef, spesso con **shōyu / mirin**	salsa dulce, generalmente con **shōyu / mirin**	molho doce do chefe, em geral com **shōyu / mirin**
Menü	pasto fisso	plato combinado	ementa fixa
kegelförmiges **Maki-zushi**	**maki-zushi** a forma di cono	**maki-zushi** en forma de cono	**maki-zushi** em forma de cone
Garnelen / Fisch / Gemüse im Backteig, frittiert	gamberetti / pesce / verdura in pastella e fritti	langostinos / pescado / verduras en gabardina crujiente, fritas	gambas / peixe / legumes fritos, envolvidos em massa
Tempura Domburi	**domburi** di **tempura**	**domburi** de **tempura**	**domburi** de **tempura**
lackierte Box mit **Tempura** + Reis	scatola laccata di **tempura** + riso	caja laqueada de **tempura** + arroz	caixa de laca de **tempura** + arroz
klare Brühe zum Tunken für **Tempura**	consommé per inzuppare **tempura**	caldo para untar **tempura**	caldo claro para molhar a **tempura**
auf heißer Platte bei Tisch gebraten	fritto su piastra calda messa sul tavolo	frito en una plancha de hierro empotrada en la mesa	frito numa placa de ferro quente na mesa
gegrillt u. mit süßer Soße glasiert	alla griglia e glassato con salsa dolce	asado a la barbacoa y glaseado con salsa dulce	grelhado e regado com molho doce
Tofu, Sojabohnenquark	semi di soia raccagliati	cuajada de semilla de soja	soja coalhada
Misosuppe mit Schweinefl. + Gemüse	minestra di **miso** con maiale + verdura	sopa de **miso** con carne de cerdo + verduras	sopa **miso** com porco + legumes
frittiertes, paniertes Schweinskotelett	cotoletta di maiale impanata e fritta	costilla de cerdo rebozada y frita	costeleta de porco panada

JAPANESE	ENGLISH	FRANÇAIS
tori-niku	chicken	poulet
tsuke-mono, -zuke	pickles in salt / vinegar / other	pickles au sel / vinaigre / autres
tsukimi	with raw egg on top (lit. full moon viewing)	servi avec œuf cru (lit. pleine lune)
tsukudani	preserves of fish / veg reduced in **shōyu + mirin**	conserves de poissons / légumes réduites dans du **shōyu + mirin**
tsuyu	stock + **shōyu**	bouillon avec **shōyu**
udon	soft, thick wheat noodles	nouilles épaisses et tendres de froment
ume-boshi	salted Japanese apricot	abricot japonais salé
una-don	charcoal-grilled eel **domburi**	**domburi** d'anguille grillé sur charbon de bois
unagi, una-	freshwater eel	anguille d'eau douce
una-jū	charcoal-grilled eel in lacquer box	anguille grillée sur charbon de bois, servie dans boîte lacquée
usutā sōsu	Japanese "Worcester sauce"	sauce brune très goûteuse
wakame	pale green flat seaweed	algues plates vert pâle
wasabi	green condiment like horseradish	raifort vert (condiment)

DEUTSCH	ITALIANO	ESPAÑOL	PORTUGUÊS
Huhn	pollo	pollo	frango
in Salz / Essig / usw. eingelegt	sottaceti in sale / aceto / altro	verduras curtidas en sal / vinagre / adobos diversos	pickles em sal / vinagre / outros
mit rohem Ei obenauf (wörtl. bei Vollmond)	con sopra uovo crudo (lett. luna piena)	con huevo crudo encima (lit. vista de luna llena)	com um ovo cru em cima (lit. vista da lua)
eingelegt. Fisch / Gemüse, in **Shōyu** + **Mirin** eingekocht	conserve di pesce / verdure ridotte in **shōyu** + **mirin**	conservas de pescado / verduras + **shōyu** + **mirin**	conservas de peixe / legumes sem molho em **shōyu** + **mirin**
Brühe + **Shōyu**	brodo + **shōyu**	caldo + **shōyu**	molho + **shōyu**
dicke, weiche Weizennudeln	spaghettoni di grano spessi e morbidi	fideos gruesos y blandos de trigo	massa de trigo espessa e macia
gesalzene japanische Aprikosen	albicocca in salamoia	albaricoque japonés salado	alperce de conserva
Domburi mit Aal vom Holzkohlengrill	**domburi** di anguilla alla brace	**domburi** de anguila a la brasa	**domburi** de enguia na brasa
Süßwasseraal	anguilla d'acqua dolce	anguila de agua dulce	enguia de água doce
Aal vom Holzkohlengrill in lackierter Box	anguilla alla brace in scatola laccata	anguila a la brasa en caja de laca	enguia na brasa, em caixade laca
japanische Würzsoße	"salsa Worcester" giapponese	salsa japonesa tipo Worcester	"molho Worcester" japonês
Wakame, hellgrüne Alge	alga marina sottile verde chiara	alga marina plana de color verde claro	alga verde pálida e lisa
wie Meerrettich	rafano giapponese	rábano picante verde	como o rábano

141

JAPANESE	ENGLISH	FRANÇAIS
wa-shoku	any traditional Japanese food	toute nourriture japonaise traditionnelle
-ya	restaurant / shop (lit. vendor)	restaurant / commerce (lit. vendeur)
yaki-mono, -yaki	grilled / shallow-fried	grillé / cuit à la poêle
yaki-niku	grilled meat, cooked at table	grillade de viande, préparée devant les convives
yaki-tori	grilled, skewered chicken pieces	brochette de poulet grillé
yakumi	relish, condiment	condiment
yasai	vegetables	légumes
yose-nabe	mixed **nabe-mono**, esp. fish / chicken / veg	**nabe-mono** varié, surtout avec poisson / poulet / légumes
yō-shoku	Japanized western food	nourriture occidentale à la japonaise
yu-dōfu	**tōfu** boiled with kelp	**tōfu** bouilli avec du varech
yū-shoku	evening meal	repas du soir
zensai	appetiser	amuse-gueule
zōsui	rice soup + meat / fish / veg	soupe de riz avec viande / poisson / légumes

DEUTSCH	ITALIANO	ESPAÑOL	PORTUGUÊS
jede trad. japanische Speise	qualsiasi cibo tradizionale giapponese	cualquier comida japonesa tradicional	qualquer comida tradicional japonesa
Restaurant / Geschäft (wörtl. Anbieter)	ristorante / negozio (lett. venditore)	restaurante / tienda	restaurante / loja (lit. vendedor)
gegrillt / i. d. Pfanne gebraten	alla griglia / saltato	asado / frito en sartén	grelhado / frito em pouca gordura
bei Tisch gegrilltes Fleisch	carne alla griglia cotta al tavolo	carne asada en la mesa	carne grelhada, cozinhada à mesa
gegrillte Hühnerstückchen am Spieß	spiedini di pollo alla griglia	brochetas de pollo a la barbacoa	churrásco de galinha no espeto
Relish	salsa piccante, condimento	salsa, condimento	condimento
Gemüse	verdure	verduras	legumes
gem. **Nabe-mono**, bes. Fisch / Huhn / Gemüse	**nabe-mono** misto, specialm. con pesce / pollo / verdura	**nabe-mono** mixto de pescado / pollo / verduras	**nabe-mono** misto, ex: peixe / frango / legumes
japanisierte westliche Speisen	cibo occidentale reso un po'giapponese	comida occidental adaptada al gusto japonés	comida ocidental à japonesa
mit Kelpalge gekochter **Tōfu**	**tōfu** bollito con alghe marine	**tōfu** hervido con algas marinas	**tofū** cozido com algas
Abendessen	cena	cena	refeição à noite
Häppchen	antipasto	aperitivo, tapa	aperitivo
Reissuppe + Fleisch / Fisch / Gemüse	minestra di riso + carne / pesce / verdura	sopa de arroz + carne / pescado / verdura	sopa de arroz + carne / peixe / legumes

Published by: Cross Media Ltd. 13 Berners Street, London W1P 4BY, UK
TEL: 020-7436-1960, FAX: 020-7436-1930 www.crossmedia.co.uk
Project manager: Kazuhiro Marumo   Editor: Jacky Rodger
Designer: Misa Watanabe   Photographer: Teruyuki Yoshimura
Translators: Christine Penman, Brigitte Scott, Alessandra Gori-MacKenzie, Ana Elisa Eskuche & Herminia Ribet, TIPS,Lda
Thanks to: Suntory Restaurant (London), Saga (London), Ramen Seto (London), Utsuwa-no-yakata (London),
Mitsuhiro Sakamoto, Nobuaki Moriyama, Yukiko Tajima   Photography and text © Cross Media Ltd. 1999 Printed in Japan
ISBN: 1 897701 96 9